Philippine Experiences

of a Kansas Farm Girl

By

Doris Imhof Johnson

Printed in the United States of America.

ISBN: 978-1-4669-1623-4 (sc)
ISBN: 978-1-4669-1625-8 (hc)
ISBN: 978-1-4669-1624-1 (e)

Library of Congress Control Number: 2012906067

Trafford rev. 04/18/2012

 www.trafford.com

North America & international
toll-free: 1 888 232 4444 (USA & Canada)
phone: 250 383 6864 ♦ fax: 812 355 4082

To my Aunt Margie Imhof, who encouraged and inspired me to take a fifty year old trip down memory lane and write a book about my experiences as a young woman traveling to the Philippines.

Preface

This book was written to share the culture, customs, and people of a truly unique and beautiful country, the Philippine Islands. After living a sheltered life of a farm girl, I embarked on a world wide adventure that would change my life and way of thinking forever. I hope this book will inspire you to think about becoming involved in a broader picture of the world and its people by traveling or reading about other countries, cultures, people, and religions.

The content of this book was gleaned from the fabulous memories I had as an IFYE. I also referred to letters written while I was in the Philippines to my boyfriend, Alvin Johnson, who later became my husband. He'd kept the letters over forty-five years. I also recorded daily activities in a journal while I was gone. These were my resource materials for this book.

The IFYE program was founded following the end of World War II as young Americans perceived the need for greater international understanding and cooperation. The first two-way exchange took place in 1948 with 17 youth from the United States. That exchange led to the development of the International Farm Youth Exchange under the auspices of the National 4-H Foundation, and later the National 4-H Council. The name was changed in 1973 to the International Four-H Youth Exchange. Exchanges have continued for more than 60 years, during that time more than 4,900 Americans have lived in 116 countries, and a like number of young people from those nations have come to the United States. Upon returning home, IFYE participants share their once-in-a-lifetime experiences with thousands of people in their communities, state, and nation.

IFYE exchanges are conducted in collaboration with participating land grant universities and are facilitated and supported by the IFYE Association of the USA and IFYE Foundation of the USA. IFYE currently has no direct ties to 4-H, as of 2006, USDA/National 4-H decided that 4-H would only support exchanges of 4-H age youth.

Today, IFYE is an international exchange program for 4-H alumni and other young adults, ages 19 to 30, interested in a rural living experience, with host families, in another country in order to promote peace through understanding. Both the IFYE and the host family learn about each other's culture and share life experiences by participating in daily life.

The IFYE vision of "World Peace through Understanding" continues to touch the lives of people around the world. IFYE alumni from other nations returned home to help develop national exchange programs and continue their ties with IFYE alumni in the United States.

Acknowledgments

I'd like to take this opportunity to "Thank" several people for helping me bring my book, *Philippine Experiences of a Kansas Farm Girl,* to fruition.

First, my brother, Ray Imhof, who patiently and steadfastly formatted, proofread, and encouraged me every step of the way while working on the book. Bets Mills, a new and dear friend in Abilene, was willing and diligent in proofreading and making suggestions for making my manuscript better. I appreciate the time and expertise she devoted in helping me.

Thank you, Alan Lambert, National IFYE Association President, who assisted in obtaining permission for me to use the IFYE logo on the back cover of my book.

The Far East IFYE delegation, who went to Japan, Taiwan, and the Philippines were supportive of my book endeavor and provided biographical information of their 'life after IFYE' found on the last few pages of this book. I'd like to "Thank" Frank Fender, Sharon Ries Brungard, Bev Malnar Morin, and Larry Hiller for writing biographical stories about their career and family.

Thank you for reading my book. I hope it will bring good cheer and happiness, as well as, "World Peace through Understanding".

IFYE
Dream Big

"Anything you can dream, you can accomplish..."

    Just what makes that little old ant think he can move a rubber tree plant? Anyone knows an ant can't move a rubber tree plant. But he's got high hope. He's got high in the sky apple pie hope.

    The words to the song, *High Hope*, were written by Sammy Cahn and Jimmy Van Heusen. It was often sung by Frank Sinatra.

    This is the kind of optimism I had.

    I sang this jaunty little song as I drove from our family farm northeast of Brewster, Kansas full of optimism and high hope. I was headed to Manhattan, 300 miles away to face an interview board in hopes of being selected as an IFYE, International Farm Youth Exchange, delegate. I knew the interview would be arduous and competitive because this ambassador program was a coveted experience among 4-Hers. Like the little old ant in the song, I had high hope and for years had dreamed of some day being selected as an IFYE ambassador to a foreign country. It really didn't matter which country they sent me to, I knew I would be a good representative for the United States. I wanted to learn about other countries, people, and cultures.

    The interview and selection process involved going before a panel of State Extension personnel and former IFYEs, who asked all sorts of questions. Primarily the questions pertained to why I thought I was qualified to be a 4-H representative to a foreign country, my thoughts about racial bias, knowledge of world affairs, knowledge of my own country, and my ability and flexibility to adapt to other people and unfamiliar customs. In essence they wanted to know if I was sincere in learning about other people and their country, as well as being able to put the United States in favorable light. We were also entertained at a banquet and a picnic to determine how well we interacted with people we didn't know and they watched our social graces or lack thereof. I must have met the test and approval of the interviewers because in a couple of weeks, I received a letter in the mail that I'd been accepted as an IFYE delegate to the

1

Philippines. I was elated. Those two weeks between the interview and receiving the letter dragged by. I scurried to the mailbox every day hoping for that letter. I remember my hands were trembling as I tore open the envelope and let out a squeal of joy. I'd been accepted.

Selected

My father was a man of few words and even fewer letters, so I was honored to receive the following letter. It came to me at college amidst my flurry of classes and final exams as I was finishing my last semester at Kansas State University. This was in regards to my being selected as an IFYE delegate. Father wrote:

May 1962

Dear Doris,

Your mother and I are very proud of you. We know you've worked hard for this award. The people in the community and the extension agents are also happy for you. I know you'll have lots of work to do in a short time with finishing college and getting ready for the trip. This is a wonderful opportunity and comes at a good time in your life. I know you will make the most of it, as you have always worked hard at whatever you set your mind to do.

Bob

After being selected, I spent a week in Washington D.C. for orientation at the National 4-H Center.

During the orientation we had some very interesting sessions. There were some on communism and racial issues. The session on communism was presented by a fellow from the

USIA, United States Information Agency. We also visited the USDA, United States Department of Agriculture, and were informed of recent developments in government and agricultural policies.

At the National 4-H Center there were incoming IFYEs, as well as those going out of the country. Some of the incoming IFYEs were from Austria, Jamaica, Germany, Spain, Czechoslovakia, Sweden, and France. They would be placed with host families throughout the United States.

INTERNATIONAL FARM
YOUTH EXCHANGE

"For a Better World
Understanding"

DORIS IMHOF
Brewster
Kansas — U.S.A.

1962 DELEGATE TO THE
PHILIPPINES

International Farm Youth Exchange

BEVERLY ANN MALNAR
Route 1
Ewen, Michigan
U.S.A.

1962 DELEGATE TO JAPAN

International Farm Youth Exchange

國際農業青年交換

For Friendship and Mutual Understanding

FRANK FENDER
RFD
GOSHEN, OHIO
U.S.A.

1962 Delegate to Taiwan

INTERNATIONAL
FARM YOUTH
EXCHANGEE

Larry Hiller
MORNING SUN, IOWA, U.S.A.

1962 Delegate to
The Philippines

INTERNATIONAL FARM YOUTH EXCHANGE
A People-to-People Program for World Understanding

DONALD MILLER
ROUTE 1. BOX 22
LOWDEN, WASHINGTON
U.S.A.

1962 Delegate
to
Japan

No Photo Available For
Sharon Reis
The Other Delegate
To Taiwan

IFYE Delegation to the Far East

Washington D.C.
National 4-H Center
June 2, 1962

Dear Al,

So much has happened in the last 48 hours, I don't know where to begin.

I had a fabulous time flying. (Doris is referring to her flight from Goodland, Kansas to Kansas City then on to Washington D.C.). Instead of having a 5 hour wait at the Kansas City Airport, it was 8 hours. The TWA flight I originally planned to go on was cancelled, so ended up going on a TWA jet, which was more fun anyway. It only cost $4.00 more. I had 1 ½ hours of sleep in the last 36 hours. I was too excited, and seeing so many things, I couldn't sleep anyway.

We got the good news yesterday that the Far East delegation (two delegates to Japan, two to the Philippines, and the two to the Republic of China) will be going to Los Angeles instead of San Francisco via bus rather than flying. Hurray—a 7 day bus trip across the U.S.

After much packing and repacking, I got my baggage weight down to 40 lbs. I don't have half as much stuff as a lot of the IFYEs have—you should see how much some of the boys have. Dad talked me out of sending any baggage on to the west coast. Sure am glad, since we won't be going to San Francisco. It would have been just sitting somewhere. I couldn't carry much more anyway.

Forty pounds are awful heavy.

(I finished my last semester at Kansas State University and was graduating with a Bachelor of Science degree in Home Economics Extension and Teaching. The graduation ceremony was in June. I missed it because I left on the IFYE trip before graduation occurred).

Guess what—you won't believe this because I haven't yet. I got an "A" in student teaching and a "B" in Food Demonstration. Haven't heard yet what grade I got in extension class or home management. I'll probably get a "C" in home management, which will take care of my "A" in student teaching.

I've got to be at another discussion session in a few minutes. I'll be thinking about you tomorrow at graduation. Am real glad your parents are going.
Love, Doris

National 4-H Center
Washington D.C.
June 3, 1962

Dear Folks,

I'm having a fabulous time. My trip to D.C. was tiring, but wonderful. Flying was quite a thrill. The flight from Goodland to K.C. was rough. It was raining and stormy most of the way. We did an unexpected landing in Hays and waited about thirty minutes for the storm to move on.

So far, I haven't seen much of D.C. They've kept us pretty busy. The six delegates going to the Far East (Japan, Republic of China, and the Philippines) will be crossing the United States by Greyhound bus instead of plane as we had thought. We will soon be en route to Los Angeles leaving here June 8th and leaving L.A. June 15th by ship. On our return trip, we are trying to make arrangements to come back through Europe.

————

I just found out, we definitely get to come back through Europe. The additional cost for each of us is $150.

Our itinerary through the U.S. is as follows:

June 8 Washington D.C. to Roanoke, Virginia
June 9 Roanoke to Knoxville, Tennessee
June 10 Knoxville to Nashville
June 11 Nashville to Texarkana, Texas
June 12 Texarkana to Sweetwater, Texas
June 13 Sweetwater through El Paso to Phoenix
June 14 Phoenix to Los Angeles We will leave Los Angeles on the ship S.S. President Cleveland, which is part of the fleet of American President Lines.

P.S. Don't worry—we have a good group and will take care of each other.

Love, Doris

Washington D.C.
National 4-H Center
June 5, 1962

Dear Al,

I'm having a ball! You know how easily and desperately I can get lost. Well, imagine finding your way around downtown Washington D.C. Sunday the IFYEs had a guided tour of D.C. Some of the things we saw were: Arlington Cemetery, National Art Gallery, White House, Senate, House of Representatives, Capitol; and Welfare, Health, and Education Department.

Larry (the other delegate to the Philippines) and I visited the Philippine Embassy this afternoon. It was very interesting. This morning we went to the Department of State Building.

Love, Doris

~~~~

National 4-H Center
Washington D.C.
June 8, 1962

Dear Al,

We are leaving here today. I am so anxious to get started. It's been fun here, but now I'm ready to go to the Philippines. Six of us are traveling together. We hope to arrive in Los Angeles June 15th, unless the Greyhound breaks down.

June 9th

This is the second day of our bus trip. We are traveling through Tennessee now. This really isn't so bad—the bus is air conditioned. We are seeing some beautiful mountainous country, and we have a swell group. The ones in our group are those going to Japan, Republic of China, and the Philippines. There are two going to each country.

Our destination today is Nashville, Tennessee.

During orientation in Washington D.C. we had some very interesting lectures. Some were on communism, that I wish you could have heard, by a fellow with USIA. We also discussed quite thoroughly the black and racial situation in the U.S.

While we were in Washington D.C., three IFYE's from Austria arrived. They were tall, nice looking, robust fellows who could speak English very well. I tried to speak to them in German. We got along fine as far as I could go. One of them was going to Little Rock, Arkansas.

There was also a very nice young lady from Jamaica who is going to Kansas as her first state. She didn't know where she would be in Kansas.

Have a good and safe trip. Keep me informed about Europe.

(Al had been accepted to participate in a program called "Classrooms Abroad" to go to Austria to study the culture and German language. He'd spend the summer there).

Love, Doris

~~~~

Phoenix, Arizona
June 14, 1962

Dear Al,

Am having a really wonderful trip and meeting some interesting people. Tomorrow ends our bus trip. I hope you got the letter I sent to New York. Let me know what you saw going across the U.S. Wish I had mentioned to try to see the Smithsonian Institute while in Washington D.C. We didn't get to see it—just didn't have time. Maybe on the way back I'll see some more of Washington D.C. and New York City. It depends on how big a hurry I am in to get home, and what my financial situation is by then.

On our bus trip across the U.S. we are each allowed $8.00 a day by the 4-H Foundation for food and room. So far we have managed to stay well within this—of course, we haven't eaten anything but sandwiches for a week. Some of the hotels we've stayed at haven't been too good either, but we're having a wonderful time. When we get to L.A. they had better watch out! After a week on a bus, we might do about anything. We are going to splurge and have a steak dinner.

The fellows in our group are very nice. We have a real good time together as IFYE brothers and sisters. Two in our group are engaged, however not to each other. They are the girl going to Japan and Larry, my IFYE brother to the Philippines. Only four of us will be coming back through Europe. The delegates to Japan are coming straight home, because Bev Is getting married and wants to plan her wedding.

So far, we've managed to keep all our baggage together. We are quite a sight with coats, suitcases, cameras, camera bags, notebooks, purses, and umbrellas.

It is really hot here in Phoenix. The bus is air conditioned, but it was still warm. All the wheat was cut in Texas. Some of it made between 40 and 50 bushels per acre. Last night at El Paso we tried some Mexican food. It was awful. We stayed in El Paso and went over into Juarez, Old Mexico. I'd been there before, but I still saw new and interesting things.

June 15th we boarded the S.S. President Cleveland ship at the Los Angeles harbor bound for Hawaii.

Love, Doris

~~~~

Honolulu, Hawaii
June 20, 1962

Dear Al,

Today we arrived in Honolulu. The ship is very nice. It's complete with swimming pool, movies (about 10 years old, but movies, nevertheless), and barber and beauty shops. The ocean has been calm and the weather is beautiful–very warm.

There are many Japanese and Filipino people on board and quite a few children, too.

The food is delicious. You might know, they are starting us out right with rice every meal. They've served rice every meal so far, except breakfast. We have been on the ship five days now. I haven't been seasick at all—feel wonderful.

Sunday church services were held. It just didn't seem like church. I know God can be worshipped any time, any place, but still the reverence and peace that should be there were gone.

To eat, we are seated at tables according to our destination. There are seven at our table—two IFYEs to the Philippines, two Filipino men going home, and three American missionaries going to Manila. Two of the missionaries, a man and his wife, have worked in the Philippines for nine years. They go back to the United States every four or five years. The other missionary is going to marry a Filipino girl as soon as he arrives.

On this ship there are 750 passengers. There are 100 students aboard going to Hawaii to study and play (mostly play) for the summer.

In our sleeping quarters there are four people. It's about a 10 x 10 ft. space—with two bunk beds and a foot locker for each person. There's also a lavatory. That's handy for puking; I guess—haven't had to use it yet. There really isn't much room, but it doesn't take much space to sleep. The ship doesn't rock around much, or maybe I'm getting used to it. It's so peaceful and nice out here—nothing but water and sky for miles and miles. The sunset, moon, and the ocean are beautiful. The water is so blue.

Love, Doris

L-R: Larry, Frank, Doris, Sharon, Bev, & Don in Hawaii

S.S. President Cleveland

June 27, 1962
Nearing Yokohama, Japan

We're still aboard the S.S. President Cleveland. Two more days and we'll arrive in Yokohama. After that, it will be another week until we reach Manila. It will seem very good to see land again and be with our host families at last.

In Honolulu we had a wonderful time. We spent most of the afternoon at Waikiki Beach. Everything in Honolulu was very expensive. I've been so hungry for watermelon. In Honolulu watermelon was 43 cents a pound. We decided we could do without for that price. We had fun slurping and um-ing over the delicious fresh pineapple.

There are quite a few little kids on the ship, needless to say, they get pretty noisy sometimes. There are also some stuffy old ladies aboard. The kids and the old ladies don't get along very well! It's a pain in the neck to listen to the old ladies complain about the noise. I hope I never get so old and crabby. After being cooped up for two weeks, I feel like hollering, too.

The food is very good, although we have chicken and apples real often—at least once a day in one form or another. We've also had all sorts of good Filipino foods such as: long rice with shrimp, dried fish about 1½ inches long served as an appetizer, crab meat and scrambled eggs, pickled green vegetables with ham. They've also served us lily root soup and calf stomach. These dishes are really pretty good, once you get up nerve enough to taste them.

There's a nice Filipino fellow on board, who has helped me a lot with Tagalog. The pronunciation isn't difficult, but the words are long, and it takes much practice to say them very fast. He is really patient and only laughs at the mistakes and awkwardness. They are amused by the American accent we put on Tagalog words.

The other day we had a navigation tour of the ship. It was really interesting and surprising to see all the instruments and gadgets it takes to keep a big ship like this going. Everything was fine until our guide said, "There are three miles of water under us." I don't believe I care for a swim.

June 28

Today is Thursday, I think. It's easy to lose track of days or time way out here in nowhere. It'll be wonderful to reach Yokohama tomorrow and be on land again for even one day. You just can't imagine unless you've been on a ship for two weeks.

After Yokohama, Larry and I will go on to Manila alone. Four of our group gets off at Yokohama. We have eight more days until we reach Manila, but really only six days on ship. We spend a day in Yokohama. We hope to go to Tokyo, which is only about twenty miles from Yokohama.

June 29, 1962

Our ship docked in Yokohama, Japan for a short time to unload and load cargo and passengers. This is where four of our IFYE companions depart, which are the two staying in Japan and the two going to the Republic of China. Larry and I will be continuing on to the Philippines. While in Yokohama, I bought some Noritake china to have shipped home. It is a service place setting of 12 with the pattern name 'Romance'. The china cost 20,000 yen or about $50.

We spent most of our time in Tokyo and saw the Imperial Palace. Tokyo is very modern. They have beautiful buildings and the architecture is out of this world. Their department stores are fabulous. Maybe we have them, but I've never seen such beautiful stores in the United States.

We'll be stopping at Hong Kong before reaching Manila.

~~~~

Excerpt from a letter/birthday card written by Esther Imhof revealing the frustrations and fears of a mother knowing her daughter is traveling halfway around the world.

July 2, 1962

Dear Doris,

The ship carries you farther away from home each day and you will soon be as far away as you can get. I remember very well twenty-two years ago today the happiness that came to your father and me in the wee hours of the morning. You arrived at 2:30 a.m. July 2, and Dad lay awake and admired you until it was time for him to go to work. He named you too, only asking my approval on the name. Well, I know this won't reach you on your birthday, but it won't be long now before you arrive in the Philippines and collect all these letters I've been sending as a means of relieving my frustration that builds up knowing you aren't there to receive them.

Love, Mom

July 4, 1962
We arrived in the Philippines.

July 8, 1962

Dear Al,

We have been in Manila four days. What a wonderful feeling to be on land again. Everything is really Americanized here in Manila. I know it won't be in the rural areas.

Larry, the other IFYE to the Philippines from Iowa, and I went to the Ellinwood-Malate church. It's a Presbyterian church and is one of the largest and most beautiful churches in Manila. We are staying in the Luneta Hotel here in Manila until we are united with our first host family.

Soon we'll be staying with our host families. We'll be with each family 3-4 weeks. The provinces where I'll be staying are: Bulacan, Palawan, Ilocos Norte, Mountain Province, Negros Oriental, Zamboanga del Sur, and Lanao del Norte. The last two provinces are on the island of Mindanao. Bulacan is just north of Manila. Palawan is another island west of the main group of islands in the South China Sea. I am the first IFYE to be sent there.

Yesterday we visited Laguna province about 130 kilometers (80 miles) south of Manila. We went by jeep, which is a typical means of transportation here. Their roads are very, very rough. We had a good glimpse of what rural Filipino life is like. Their homes and farming methods are quite primitive, but well adapted to the climate and peoples' needs. The countryside is beautiful—just covered with vegetation—mostly coconut trees. We saw rice paddies, corn fields, and sugar cane.

Every place we went the people stared and children gathered around to get a closer look, and some even touched the 'Americanos'. They were amazed to see such tall, white people.

Most people in the Philippines can speak English. Many are embarrassed or ashamed that they can't speak very well, so prefer Tagalog, their national language. Especially, the older people are hesitant to speak English.

It's the beginning of the rainy season here, so every day it rains several times, not just a sprinkle either, but a downpour.

Last night some places here in Manila had three feet of flood water in the streets. We are on the edge of tropical storm, Joan. It's very hot here. I don't know how to describe this kind of heat. I've never experienced anything like it. When people's faces and arms are always wet with perspiration, and you can feel sweat trickle down your back, you know it's hot.

Al, don't become discouraged about the language barrier in Austria. As for the cultural differences, they told us at orientation to try to determine why there are differences and also to look for similarities.

Paalam (Good-bye in Tagalog)
Love, Doris

~~~~

The following are some newspaper stories I sent home while in the Philippines as an IFYE. They were published in the Colby Free Press in Colby, Kansas.

Published Monday, Sept. 3, 1962

Greetings from the Philippines:

Many wonderful and exciting things have happened since my plane departed May 31 from the Kansas City airport for Washington, D.C. Thirty IFYEs gathered at Washington, D.C. for one week orientation program before leaving for their respective countries. After the orientation, six of us (the delegates to Japan, Republic of China, and the Philippines) started across the United States via Greyhound bus for Los Angeles. In spite of the long hours of riding on the bus, we had a good time seeing the country. On June 15th we sailed from Los Angeles on the ship, President Cleveland. The three week voyage was packed with fun. Many hours were spent lying in the sun and conversing with friends from Japan, China, and the Philippines. The ship was well equipped with all sorts of recreational facilities—dance band, movies, books, games, swimming pool, and refreshment stand. Along the way we stopped in Honolulu, Yokohama, Saigon, and Hong Kong. We had a fabulous time seeing the sights, riding in the rickshaws, and trying to speak Japanese.

15

Finally, we arrived in Manila July 4th. Although the ship had been a wonderful experience, I was glad to set my feet on land again.

We spent a week in Manila making courtesy calls to important officials. These included the Secretary of Agriculture, AID, USIS, American Embassy, and becoming acquainted with Extension workers at the Bureau of Agricultural Extension. At the orientation in Manila, I learned I would be living in seven provinces with seven families during my six month stay here. This allows approximately a three week stay with each family. In this time I will have a chance to visit four of the larger islands in the Philippines: Luzon, Palawan, Mindanao, and Negros. The entire Philippine archipelago consists of 7,100 islands.

On July 13th I was filled with excitement and anticipation as we made our way to Malolos, Bulacan, where I would be living with my first host family. Bulacan is a province just north of Manila. A province is equivalent to a state, although Bulacan's land area is about the size of only two counties.

The Filipino families are quite large—ranging from 6 to 13 children. In some instances, the family consists of Inang (mother), Tatang (father), children, auntie, and grandparents. In all cases, the oldest man in the house is head of the household, which is frequently grandfather. Mother is always the family treasurer.

After two weeks, I am living with my third host family in the province of Bulacan. During my first two weeks of actually living as a Filipino, there are two outstanding incidents I would like to share with you. These are typhoon Kate and rice culture.

Shortly after our arrival, I was told the "rainy season" had just begun. Here the rainy season begins the first part of June and continues until September. The annual rainfall is 80-100 inches. I'm beginning to comprehend these figures now. It has rained almost continuously for five days—the beginning of typhoon Kate. Flood conditions here in Bulacan have destroyed 10,000 hectares or 25,000 acres of crops and fish ponds. The homes in most of Malolos, the capital city of Bulacan, are flooded. My host family's home in Malolos luckily is elevated, as are most of the homes, so the water is not coming into the house. The water in our front yard is knee high or about two feet deep. We've been having a delightful time wading. Yesterday my host brothers, sisters, and I made a raft of bamboo and banana tree trunks. It's really a thrilling experience to float down the street on a raft.

The children also have so much fun swimming in the streets, and are even happier, because they have no school during the flood. The water is deep enough that we can also ride in a banca, a long narrow boat carved from light weight wood.

Here in the Philippines it can rain any time with little or no warning so everyone carries an umbrella or raincoat. Because of the many rains, we go barefoot; or we wear slip-on wooden or plastic shoes, which enables our feet to dry off between rains.

My second host father helped educate me on the process of planting and milling rice. It's a long, tedious operation and involves hours of back-breaking labor on the part of the farmer. About 6:30 one morning, my host father and I visited the rice fields. Already, the families were hard at work.

My host father told me that rice is called "palay" from the time it's in the seedling stage until after it is milled. Only after it has gone through the hulling, cleaning, and polishing process is the palay called rice.

The most land that one farmer can care for by himself is two or three hectares (five to seven acres). All of the field work is done by man power with the aid of the carabao (work horse of the Philippines).

Rice culture begins with the flooded palay seed beds where rice seeds are planted very close together and allowed to grow for about four weeks. After this time the palay seedlings are pulled up, the tops cut off, and they are tied in bundles ready to be transplanted. The bundles of palay seedlings look much like bundles of green garden onions.

The fields are prepared for the young palay seedlings by plowing, harrowing, and flooding the ground. The plowing and harrowing are done by the use of handmade tools drawn by carabao.

The water is held in the rice fields by the ingenious construction of dikes built by the farmer. I observed a farmer restoring his dikes in order to conserve the water. In his particular area, no irrigating is done; so his dikes had to be very strong in order to catch and save all the rainfall. The dikes around the hillside look much like the terraces on farms at home. Construction of the dikes is done by hand. The farmer carefully and laboriously packs mud in a ridge high enough to hold the water in his fields. The dike is approximately two feet high. After several hard rains, he has to begin all over again rebuilding the dikes.

All members of the family—men, women, and children—help plant palay seedlings after the field is properly prepared. The planting is done by hand. The workers stand side by side across the field. Each person sets about four or five plants (each plant approximately 30 inches apart). The planters move backwards forming long rows the width of the field.

After the seedling stage, rice matures much like wheat—it takes about three to four months, depending on the variety of palay before it is ready to harvest. The palay grows to about the height of wheat and has a head in which the rice forms.

As of yet, I have not observed the harvesting of rice—most of the rice now is still in the seed beds or transplanting stage.

My host father and I also visited a rice mill where we saw many sacks of palay from last season's crop stacked and waiting to be milled. In the milling process, the hulls of the rice (similar to the hull around a kernel of wheat) are removed. Also, the palay runs through a cleaning and polishing machine. The finished product is rice.

Sacks of Rice Going to Market

Banaue Rice Terraces

There is an area north of Manila, in the mountains of Cordillera and Ifugao province, where the rice terraces are known as the 'Eighth Wonder of the World'. These terraces were carved into the mountains over 2,000 years ago by the Ifugao tribe; indigenous people of the Philippines. The Banaue terraces are approximately 5,000 feet above sea level and cover 4,000 square miles. The early tribes carved the terraces out of the sides of the mountains with their bare hands and crude implements. The terraces are still used today. They are watered by an ancient irrigation system from the rainforests above the terraces. The terraces were implemented because there was very little level ground in that area for growing rice.

In my next letter to you I will describe the food and homes of the Filipino people.

Paalam (good-bye) for now from
Your IFYE to the Philippines – Doris Imhof

2nd letter home for publication: Sept. 22, 1962

Are you ready? Fasten your seat belt. We are going to fly to Palawan, an island 365 miles southwest of Manila. Palawan is situated with the South China Sea on the west and Sulu Sea to the east.

Looking down from the plane you can see field after field of coconut trees. The straight rows really look nice. Some of the larger coconut plantations have as many as 39,000 trees.

We are arriving in Puerto Princesa, the capital of Palawan. The population of this sea coast city is 29,000. It doesn't seem like such a large city, because the streets are wide and free from the congestion of automobiles, and the homes are far apart.

Since most of the people either ride bicycles or walk, Puerto Princesa is a very quiet city. It is also very beautiful; being surrounded on the south, west, and north by tree covered mountains and to the east by the Sulu Sea.

Come now, and let's visit the home of my host parents, Governor and Mrs. Paredes, here in Puerto Princesa. The house is very large (three story) and is made of beautiful brick. It is located only about one-fourth mile from the shore of the Sulu Sea.

There are nine children in my host family. The children range in age from 18 years to a little baby boy only a few weeks old.

Downstairs is the living room, my host father's office, the dining room, and kitchen. Upstairs are the bedrooms and bathroom.

Let's stop next in the kitchen. Here, the dish washing is done with water carried from a pump outside. Food and dishes are also stored here. Actual cooking of the food is done in a separate building at the rear of the house. Also, the servants live there.

In the living room, the furniture is made of bamboo; because bamboo is very plentiful here. It is also comfortable in the warm climate.

The floors throughout the house are highly polished smooth red brick. The Filipinos have very effective floor polishers; a man-powered coconut shell, which has been cut in half. The coconut shell is placed with the cut edge next to the floor and pushed many times over the floor with the bare foot.

At the close of day, the family members retire about 8:30 or 9:00 p.m. My younger brothers and sisters sleep on woven mats on the floor; but the older children and my parents have regular beds. After a busy day, we quickly fall asleep under mosquito nets; only to be awakened early (5:30 to 6:00 a.m.) by the rising sun and crowing rooster.

Such is life in the city. Now, let's visit a farm family.

The farm homes are constructed of bamboo with nipa leaves for the roof. Unlike city homes, rural homes are usually elevated and the floors are made of bamboo slats. The house is approximately six feet off the ground. This allows air to circulate and serves as a cooling system. Dirt which accumulates on the floor can easily be removed by allowing it to fall between the cracks of the bamboo slats. The space under the house is used for storing farm implements and firewood or housing the carabao, chickens, or pigs.

Both rural and city homes have large window areas—often unscreened. The windows slide horizontally and the panes are made of shell.

Rural homes usually have outdoor toilets. Few rural areas have electricity so family member either go to bed early or use kerosene lamps.

I hope you have enjoyed your visit to Filipino homes. You will find they are comfortable and well suited to the climate here. The natural resources are well utilized in construction of the home.

Next time we will sample Filipino food. My hospitality to you is poor because a Filipino will never let you leave his home without first having you join him in merienda (snack).

Bye for now. (Paalam)
Your IFYE to the Philippines
Doris Imhof

3rd letter home: October 24, 1962

Doris Imhof Writes and Describes
Favorite Foods in Philippine Islands

Come with me. I want you to taste some of the Filipino foods.
Leave your calorie book at home, enjoy the food, and eat plenty.
That's what I've done. The result? Ten additional pounds around
my waist, but what an enjoyable way to gain weight.

One of the most delicious desserts made here is called
leche-flan. It is a type of custard and is made either with canned
milk or fresh carabao milk. To make it even richer and more
delicious, only the egg yolk is used. Leche-flan is cooked by
steaming for about one to one and a half hours.

I want to tell you of my experience trying to eat balut. My
first host father was anxious for me to taste this. The lady selling
balut came past our house about 10 o'clock at night. Balut is a
chicken or duck egg which as been incubated 18 days. When the
balut vendor came, my father bought four eggs. He
demonstrated how balut is eaten and enjoyed. After he had
eaten three eggs, it was my turn. My family really laughed at
seeing me trying to eat balut. I guess it was the idea of eating a
whole baby chick that kept me from enjoying it like my father had.
Of course, balut is perfectly clean and thoroughly cooked. It is
prepared much like a hard boiled egg. The eggs are savored for
their texture and flavor. The broth surrounding the embryo is
sipped from the shell before the egg is peeled, and then the yolk
and young chick can be eaten. The chick inside the balut is not
old enough to show its beak, feathers, or claws and the bones
are undeveloped. Balut is not exclusive to the Philippines. Other
Asian countries such as Cambodia, China, and Vietnam also
include balut in their diets.

Since there is no winter here in the Philippines or frost which
would destroy vegetation, there is an abundance of fresh fruits
and vegetables all year. Thus, there is little need for food
preservation.

I've found that foods in different provinces vary depending on
the availability, so it is difficult to describe all foods of the
Philippines.

One of my favorite Ilocano dishes (Ilocano region is that in northern Luzon) is pinachet. Pinachet is similar to stew in the U.S. The ingredients include small eggplants, ampalaya (a squash-like vegetable), leaves and blossoms of camote (a sweet potato plant), green peppers, green beans, and onions.

How about some roast pork (lecion)? A whole butchered pig four or five months old is the ideal size for the tastiest lecion. A green bamboo stalk about seven feet long is inserted lengthwise through the pig. After the pig is on the pole, it is ready to be turned slowly over an outdoor fire for two to four hours. It is roasted slowly so the interior is well done, while the outside skin becomes browned and very crisp.

Before the pig is placed on the pole, it is stuffed with tamarin leaves which add seasoning. During roasting, flavor and aroma from the leaves penetrate through the meat.

Rice, here in the Philippines, is eaten three times a day. It is usually boiled, although sometimes fried rice is served for breakfast. Rice is used much like bread is used in the U.S.

The custom here of having mid-morning and afternoon snacks (merienda) is similar to the American habit. Calamansi juice (similar to lemonade), Coca Cola, or coffee is usually served. Often, cookies, rice cake, fruit, or ice cream is served at this time. It is part of Filipino hospitality to offer a visitor something to eat. So, if you visit six homes you have six meriendas.

The usual Filipino meal consists of rice, fish, chicken, fresh fruits, cooked vegetables, and soup. Beverages are not included with the meal, but are served with dessert.

Maybe you are less hungry now. Before you leave, I must tell you about adobo. This is an everyday food which is eaten throughout the Philippines. Adobo is made with either pork or chicken. The meat is fried, after first being tenderized with calamansi juice. It is cooked with onion, garlic, green pepper, and tomato.

I hope you have enjoyed sampling Filipino food.

Your IFYE to the Philippines
Doris Imhof

4th letter home: Dec. 3, 1962

Dear Friends,

Magandang umaga (Good Morning).

It's a beautiful day in the Philippines. Although it's early, people have been up a long time preparing for the barrio (rural community) fiesta in honor of the patron saint. During the fiesta, many friends and relatives from neighboring barrios and towns come to eat and visit with families in the barrio holding the fiesta.

Regardless of whether you know the family or not, during fiesta time, you can go to their home and eat. The feasting and activities of the day begin early and last late; the custom being to go from house to house seeing friends and eating at each house. At the fiesta I attended, we ate eight or ten times.

Since the fiesta is a gala occasion held annually, plans for next year's fiesta are in the making almost before this year's fiesta is over.

There are many jobs to be performed in preparation for the fiesta. In the weeks before, the families are all busy making necessary repairs on their home, cleaning the yard, and doing 'spring house cleaning'. Also, chickens, pigs, goats, and cows are being fattened for the food during the fiesta.

All families in the barrio look ahead to the time of fiesta by saving food and money throughout the year. A common expression here is: "We Filipinos work and save all year only to spend everything in one day." This is true, but the people are very happy and really look forward to their fiesta with great excitement and anticipation. It is estimated that the minimum a family spends for the fiesta is 100 pesos ($25). Many mayors are encouraging the people to spend less, because often money which should be used for food, clothing, and education is spent during the fiesta.

The day and night before the fiesta, the cries and sounds of the animals can be heard throughout the barrio as they are being slaughtered in preparation for the next day. As well as preparing enough food for the many people who will visit their home, each family prepares food for their friends to take home with them when they leave. This is called 'bring house'.

Besides eating and visiting, there are other activities: such as volleyball and other outdoor sports, cockfighting, a parade honoring the patron saint, gambling games, dancing, and singing.

Cockfighting is legal and a national sport among the Filipinos. The cocks are equipped with a razor sharp blade on each leg. Then, they are put in a ring (called a cockpit) and proceed to fight until one is killed or runs away. The cocks are trained by their owners to be aggressive. Much betting is done, and the people are really enthusiastic. The owner of the winning cock receives money, as well as the spectators who have placed bets on the winning cock. It is a fight to the bloody end. The noise in the cockfighting pit is similar to cheering at a basketball game. Records show cockfighting existed as early as 1837.

In the afternoon of the fiesta, there is a parade honoring the patron saint. A band plays, and many people form a procession as they follow a statue of the patron saint. Each family places candles in the windows of their home. These are lighted as the procession passes the house. This is a way of honoring or paying respect to the patron saint of that barrio. A patron saint is an intercessor believed to be able to intercede effectively for the needs of their special charges. The patron saint is the heaven's advocate for a nation, place, craft, activity, class, clan, family, or person. Each town or barrio has a different day on which they celebrate their fiesta, depending on the patron saint they are honoring. The fiesta is a custom established in the Philippines during the 400 years of Spanish influence.

On the evening of the fiesta there is a big dance. Usually, a queen is selected from among the young girls to represent the beauty of the barrio and to reign over the dance. There is much merry-making, and the dances are lively.

A fiesta is an interesting and enjoyable day for everyone. I went home feeling very tired and 'busog' (full) after the day of feasting; but really satisfied and happy for having learned about this unique custom of the Philippines.

Bye for now,
Your IFYE to the Philippines
Doris Imhof

5th letter home for publication: Dec. 20, 1962

Dear Friends,

Greetings from Lanao, Moroland of the Philippines. This is the province of Muslims (Moros), the non-Christian natives. The people here do not like to be called Moro, because it means "savage". I am living now with my 7th and last host family, one of the few Christian families in this area.

I have been very fortunate to live in Muslim communities and observe their way of life. Here, the Muslim people are considered by the modern Filipino as being equivalent to our early American Indian. The Muslims also form tribes, and sometimes go on the warpath. The less-educated Muslims believe it is not a sin to kill their fellowmen.

One day, my host mother said, "Would you like to attend a Muslim mass?" I was delighted and also a little frightened. On Friday, which is the day of worship for Muslims, we went to their mosque.

Here, I was surprised to see the men and women washing themselves—their face, arms, head, and feet. This is to cleanse their thoughts, body, and spirit. Then, if on their way to the chapel, anyone touches them, they return again to the spring to wash.

Before entering the chapel we removed our shoes. After going inside, the men removed their trousers and placed around themselves a piece of cloth similar to a tablecloth called 'malong'. They do not like to worship in the same clothes worn for working in the fields, so their work clothes are replaced with the 'malong', which they know is clean.

The service consisted of a series of chants and singing conducted in the Muslim vernacular (one of the approximately 170 dialects of the Philippines). The men knelt on the floor in the front of the chapel and the women behind. My father jokingly said, "They do this so the men can concentrate on the prayer instead of being distracted by the attractive ladies."

The reason there are so many dialects is that the islands are surrounded by water, which isolates groups of people. These groups have formed their own unique language within their geographical area. Thus, many dialects exist in the Philippines, besides 8 major languages which are: Tagalog, Ilokano, Cebuano, Kapampangan, Hiligaynon (Ilonggo), Waray, Bikolano, and Pangasinan. Spanish was the official language for the 400 years the Spaniards colonized the Philippines. The languages being taught in Philippine schools today are Tagalog and English.

Later, we were invited to have lunch with a group of farmers from the Muslim community. The main dish of the meal was curried goat. Goat is a popular meat among the Muslim people, because they do not eat pork. It is against their religion to eat pork. Eating the flesh of the pig to them is unsanitary.

Because the Muslim religion and customs are unique, for many years these people have separated themselves from the Christians. Muslims are definitely the minority group here in the Philippines. As Christians settled on the island of Mindanao, the Muslims moved farther into the mountains.

Now, the Muslims are becoming more progressive and integrating with their Christian countrymen. I was happy to learn that one of the IFYEs from the Philippines to the United States this year is a Muslim from Lanao.

This experience has helped me understand and appreciate the religions of other people.

In my next letter I'll share with you a variety of experiences I've had working with Filipino farm families.

So long for now.
Your IFYE to the Philippines
Doris Imhof

Final letter home for publication:
Aboard the S.S. Vietnam
December 28, 1962

Dear Friends,

This will be the last of a series of letters I've written telling of experiences during my six month stay in the Philippines. I am en route home now. We are nearing the Suez Canal and will soon be arriving in Marseille, France. By January 18th, I will be home, and am looking forward to talking to many of you personally and showing my pictures of the Philippines.

As we are cruising through the Mediterranean Sea, I'll reminisce about some of the last experiences I had in the Philippines. As I have been reminiscing about the Filipino homes and families, I have recalled many cultural similarities.

I remember one day in August with my second host family. It was very hot. Mother and I had prepared an afternoon snack and just sat down to relax and enjoy it. Only then, did we realize the countless number of flies hovering around the table. Yes, people in other countries are also plagued with flies and many kinds of insects. I was astonished when my host mother turned to me and asked, "Do you have flies in the U.S.?"

Farmers all over the world have basically the same hopes, ideals, and fears. Why do I say this? I want you to observe my third host father, who grew rice, garlic, sugar cane, and tobacco on his farm. While I lived with them, I had a chance to share the fears and anxieties connected with the approaching rice harvest. Several times a day, my host father would inspect and look at his ripening rice to make sure it was not being invaded by rice stem

30

borers or being blown down by strong winds and rain of the typhoons. He also counted the number of rice kernels in each panicle (head) trying to estimate the yield. His actions and anticipations of the forthcoming harvest reminded me of my father and the neighbors at home during the approaching wheat harvest. Although crops grown and methods of farming are different, the dreams and hardships of a farmer are universal.

Tonight let's join the teenagers in their "jam session". There will be plenty of the latest dances. I'm sure you will be reminded of teen dances in the U.S. when you see our Filipino friends doing the twist, mashed potato, and jitter bug. Another favorite is the "slow drag" at which time the fellow has the opportunity to dance cheek to cheek with the girl of his choice.

You will notice that although 10,000 miles of water and land separate the United States and the Philippines, there are many familiar sights. Right now my Filipino friend is saying, as he swerves the jeep to miss a chuck hole, "Our roads here in the Philippines are first class terrible. I'll bet there are no bumpy and dusty roads like this in the states." I was quick to assure him all of our roads in the United States aren't asphalt; and we, too, have bumpy roads.

Are you thirsty after the long dusty ride? Never fear, in spite of the fact that the surroundings are very desolate looking, you have that feeling of being "miles from nowhere", and being unable to speak the native dialect; merely utter the words "Coca Cola", and you will soon be presented that magically refreshing liquid, just like that found all over the U.S. and other parts of the world. Filipinos young and old enjoy Coca Cola. It is plentiful all over the Philippines and inexpensive—about 5 cents a bottle.

As we bump along, look over there to your right towards that little rural school house. It's late afternoon and school has just been dismissed for the day. Say, that looks like my brother, Fred and his friends. What are they doing? They have gathered for a few minutes for a friendly game of marbles, and some of the more mischievous lads are threatening the girls with sling shots.

As we pass by the village on the way home, notice the men and women clustered here and there exchanging the latest bits of news and gossip. Just like home, the people in the Philippines, love to visit with their friends and neighbors discussing crops, homemaking, the cute tricks of the dela Cruz baby, cockfighting, and the weather.

Come to our home. I want you to share a quiet evening with my family. After supper the family gathers around the kerosene lamp for an evening of relaxation and chatting after the long day of work. This scene reminds me of many American families. Mother is busy darning socks and sewing buttons on Fred's shirt, which were yanked off at school during a friendly scuffle. Dad is engrossed in the daily paper. Suddenly, he and mother begin discussing the world situation; present price of rice, and the upcoming marriage of Jose San Juan's (neighbor's) daughter. What are the activities of the children tonight? Oh my, there is my studious sister, Erlinda. She is very busy doing her homework. It is her ambition to achieve honors in her class. She is studying very diligently, but is puzzled now as she asks; "How do you spell 'occasionally'? One 's' or two?"

Well, my brother and I aren't quite as ambitious, so we are having a leisurely game of checkers. It seems that checkers are played the same all over the world, and I'm as easily beaten in the Philippines as in the U.S.

On another evening, you may see father and the whole family enjoying a game of "Scrabble". I found this is an excellent means of increasing my English and Tagalog (the Filipino national language) vocabulary. The younger children are quite absorbed with a stack of comic books. Before retiring, please join our family for a before bed snack. Tonight we're having a family favorite—pomelo. Pomelo is a type of fruit similar to grapefruit, but larger and much sweeter.

No doubt, during this evening of sharing activities and experiences, you have felt, as our Filipino family does, a great deal of "togetherness". Only by sharing and understanding the similarities and differences in culture, and understanding family members, can we hope to develop world understanding.

Sincerely,
Your 1962 IFYE to the Philippines
Doris Imhof

Mancala Game

One of my host families gave me mancala, which is a family game that originated in Africa and Asia. It's sometimes called the 'sowing' or 'count and capture' game. My mancala game is wooden and carved from native Philippine wood. It has seven holes on each side with a bin at each end and is played using cowry shells. The game is for two players and each has his respective side of the board. The object of the game is to capture the opponent's shells, make it impossible for him to make any more moves, or to have his side of the board empty of shells.

Ancient players of mancala made indentations in the dirt or stone and used seeds, beans, stones, or other small objects as the pieces to be moved and placed in the holes. It has been recorded that people played mancala as early as the 17th century.

Geographical and Early History of the Philippines:

The Philippines is made up of 7,100 islands in its vast archipelago. It is located east of Vietnam between the Pacific Ocean and the South China Sea.

The people are mainly Spanish and Tagalog speaking, but each island has its own dialect. The younger generations speak English, also.

The religion is predominantly Catholic, because of early Spanish influence.

The Philippines was controlled by a number of different countries over the years, including: Spain, Japan, and the United States.

Prior to the Spanish-American War, the Philippines were a colony of Spain. After that the Philippines came under the control of the United States until Japan invaded during WW II.

Between 1942 and 1944 the Philippines were occupied by the Japanese army and their rule. A World War II American hero to the Filipino people was General Douglas MacArthur who said, "I shall return". He did just that and helped the Filipino people. They never forgot him. In 1944, General MacArthur helped clear the Philippines of the Japanese army. The Philippines was granted its independence in 1946. The Republic of the Philippines was proclaimed on July 4, 1946.

While I was in the Philippines, Diosdado P. Macapagal was President. He was President from 1961-1965. He and his wife lived in the Presidential residence called Malacanang Palace. During President Macapagal's term in office, Ferdinand Marcos was a Senator from 1959-1965.

Malacanang Palace

After returning home, it was Ferdinand Marcos whom I heard the most about in the news. He became the 10th President of the Philippines, and served from 1965-1986. He was the only President to hold two terms in office. He and his wife, Imelda Marcos, were very extravagant; while many of the Philippine people lived in poverty. Mrs. Marcos allegedly owned 5,000 pair of shoes, and all the other accessories and clothes to go with them. These two, while living in the Presidential mansion, let government pilfering run rampant among elected officials, while participating in it themselves. The Marcos' were accused of political corruption and embezzling billions of dollars from the government and the people of the Philippines. Eventually, Ferdinand Marcos and Imelda went into exile in Hawaii, where he lived until his death in 1989. His wife still lives there today. I'm not sure what happened to her 5,000 pair of shoes.

Bataan Death March

All was not fun and entertainment for us IFYEs in the Philippines, as we listened with horror while the older Filipinos related their stories of the Bataan Death March.

At dawn on April 9, 1942, against the orders of Generals Douglas MacArthur and Jonathan Wainwright, Major General Edward P. King Jr., surrendered more than 77,000 (67,000 Filipinos and 10,000 Americans) starving and disease ridden men. As it turned out, it was either surrender or be killed, because the U.S. military was vastly out-numbered. General MacArthur and Wainwright were in Australia, and didn't realize the severity of the military's situation in the Philippines. General King inquired of Colonel Motoo Nakayama, the Japanese colonel to whom he tendered his pistol in lieu of his lost sword, whether the Americans and Filipinos would be well treated. The Japanese aide-de-camp replied, "We are not barbarians". The majority of the prisoners of war were immediately robbed of their keepsakes and belongings and forced to endure a 61 mile (98 km) march in deep dust, over vehicle-broken macadam roads, and crammed into rail cars to captivity at Camp O'Donnell. Thousands died en route from disease, starvation, dehydration, heat prostration, untreated wounds, and wanton execution. The number of deaths that took place in the internment camps from delayed effects of the march is uncertain, but believed to be high.

Those few, who were lucky enough to travel to San Fernando on trucks, still had to endure more than 25 miles of marching. Prisoners were beaten randomly, and were often denied food and water. Those, who fell behind, were usually executed or left to die. Witnesses say those who broke rank for a drink of water were executed, some even decapitated. Subsequently, the sides of the roads became littered with dead bodies and those begging for help.

On the Bataan Death March approximately 54,000 of the 77,000 prisoners reached their destination. The death toll of the march is difficult to assess, as thousands of captives were able to escape from their guards. All told, approximately 5,000-10,000 Filipinos and 600-650 American prisoners of war died before they could reach Camp O'Donnell.

It was heart-wrenching to listen, as elderly Filipinos recalled having gone to the route of the Death March trying to aid their loved ones by giving them food or water. They looked on as their loved ones were murdered, and often, those offering assistance were beaten and killed, also. Such atrocities are hard to fathom.

War Crime Trial

After the surrender of Japan in 1945, an Allied commission convicted General Homma of war crimes, including the atrocities of the death march out of Bataan, and the following atrocities at Camp O'Donnell and Cabanatuan. The general, who had been absorbed in his efforts to capture Corregidor after the fall of Bataan; claimed, in his defense, that he remained ignorant of the high death toll of the death march until two months after the event. He was executed April 3, 1946 outside Manila. For unknown reasons, the Allies did not attempt to prosecute Masanobu Tsuji for war crimes.

Host Families and Itinerary
While Staying in the Philippines

1st Host Family July 13-18, 1962
Mr. and Mrs. Pacifico Bautista
Provincial Agriculturist
Malolos, Bulacan
Children: Greg, Elpie, Baby, Jr., and Caring

2nd Host Family July 18-25
Mr. and Mrs. Ciriaco Santos
Attorney
Pandi, Bulacan
Children: Fred, Noli, Boyette, and Cecil

Pandi, Philippines
July 18, 1962

Dear Al,

I am with my second host family. I'll be here only 7 days, which is certainly too short a time. My father is a very prosperous man. He's co-owner of a resort here in Pandi, founder of the high school; manager of an electric company, lawyer, and his wife is a pharmacist. There are six children ranging in age from 4-14. I like them very much, especially Noli, the 4 year old. He talks to me in Tagalog.

My first host parents were also wonderful. I stayed there only five days, but became very fond of them and their family. They had five children. There were two fine host brothers ages 20 and 22. Father is an agriculturist: a very educated man, and had been to the United States in 1960.

Love, Doris

July 20, 1962

It is the rainy season here now, and when they say rain, they mean RAIN. It has rained for two days and nights now without stopping. Most of Manila is flooded with 3-4 feet of water in the streets. I was supposed to go to Manila tomorrow for a wedding, but don't think I'll be going now. My host brother, Alfredo (14 years old) told me that sometimes they have a siyam-siyam (literally means nine-nine) and that is continuous rain for nine days and nine nights. Maybe that's what we're having now.

Yesterday, I visited the schools here in Pandi—the elementary, middle school, and high school. My host father is the organizer of the 4-H club and, since he is also manager of the school, 4-H is compulsory in high school.

3rd Host Family July 25-Aug.3
Cenon R. Florcruz
Malolos, Bulacan

August 2

Dear Al,

In this province, I have stayed with three families, and now am back again with my first host family for a short visit before leaving. We've been staying up very late (11:30 p.m.), and getting up at 6 or 6:30.

We experienced a flood here in Malolos, Bulacan. Water was knee deep in our front yard. This was because of a typhoon. Many acres (25,000) of rice and fish ponds were destroyed. The worst of the typhoon was in this province and the neighboring one to the west. Homes were evacuated and people drowned. Well, these people are taking good care of me, and I have nothing to worry about.

Today, for the first time in three weeks, I am staying home with my host mother, and have a little time to visit with her and catch up on correspondence. The people here, in their desire to make my stay enjoyable and educational, don't realize that I get tired of going so many places each day. Al, you can't imagine! And, every place we go they serve us food!

40

I'm glad I have a good appetite and strong stomach, or I'd have been sick before now.

Yesterday I talked to a group, Irrigation Association, on irrigation in the United States. I'm not an expert on irrigation, but these people think I'm a Jack-of-all-Trades. So far, I've given on the average of one or two talks a day on various subjects: 4-H, life in the U.S., American schools, extension work to women's clubs, 4-H groups, schools, faculty members, Rotary, and Lions. Every municipality we go to, I meet the mayors and other city officials. Well, so much for the necessary formalities expected of an IFYE.

Very soon now, probably tomorrow or the next day, I'll be leaving for my next province, Palawan. It is an island in the South China Sea 365 miles from here. I'll be flying there.

You asked about the bath facilities here. We bathe every day. It's with cold water: either an improvised shower or a sponge bath; nevertheless, a much appreciated bath after a long day of perspiring and dust.

Most people here speak English, if they will. Many are embarrassed or ashamed that they can't speak English very well, so prefer Tagalog.

The temperature here is 85-90 degrees, which doesn't sound very hot, but is quite miserable because of the high humidity.

Love, Doris

~~~~

Marilyn Monroe Dies

One of the news stories that made headlines around the world while I was in the Philippines was Marilyn Monroe's death. Her photo and story were splashed across the front page of every paper in the world. August 5, 1962 – "Marilyn Monroe dies at age 36." The name her parents gave her was, Norma Jeane Mortenson, but she also went by Norma Jeane Baker. The news of her death stunned the world, because everyone loved this sexy, blonde bomb shell. She was a famous singer, model, and actress. Some of the movies she starred in were: Gentlemen

Prefer Blondes, How to Marry a Millionaire, The Seven Year Itch, Bus Stop, and Some Like It Hot.

Other sad news that reached me while I was halfway around the world was the tragic automobile accident that my lifelong friend and her family were involved in at the edge of Brewster, Kansas. In the accident, my friend, Evelyn Hoyt, along with her mother and father, were hit by a vehicle that failed to stop at a stop sign. Evelyn escaped with injuries, her mother sustained serious injuries, and Evelyn's father, Ernie was killed. This was a very sad blow, because Ernie was like a second father to me.

~~~~

Manila
August 5, 1962

Dear Al,

I am staying in Manila for a few days until a plane leaves for Palawan. I was supposed to have left yesterday, but the plane was full, so will go either tomorrow or Tuesday.

You asked how I like Filipino boys. Maybe I shouldn't be so truthful, but I like them very much. They are very handsome with their dark skin, black hair, and shining brown eyes. Most of them aren't as tall as I am, but some are. They're polite and happy people. People here are very anxious to marry their eligible son to an American. It really is an embarrassing situation. When I spoke to the Rotary, they asked if I had any objections to marrying a Filipino. Oh boy! Such questions are a little touchy to answer. That is a common question. My reply is, "Marriage isn't in the guidelines of the IFYE program." That usually stops those kinds of questions.

They have some delicious candy here made from carabao milk. It's the consistency of fudge, except it is white. It's very good—also fattening.

Must get to bed now. It's late, and I have to get up at 5 a.m. to catch the plane.

Love, Doris

4th Host Family Aug. 4-25

Gov. and Mrs. Telesforo Paredes
Puerto Princesa, Palawan
Children: Emma, Jing, Estrella, Arlyn, Virgil, Gladys, Ray Dean, Jr.
and Elizabeth

Aug. 15, 1962:
Dear Al,

Greetings from Palawan. This is the second province that I'm staying in. I've been here a little over a week. My host father is the Governor of Palawan. The family is wonderful—9 children including a little baby brother only 10 days old.

I was somewhat disappointed with the extension people for placing me with the wealthier and more prominent families; but they say this is necessary for my safety and health precautions. Also, lower and middle class families can not afford to have me in their home. I was surprised to learn many people have barely enough food for their own children,

43

but the families are very large. The minimum number of children in a family is usually 6, and often as many as 12 and 13. People often ask me what suggestions I would have to help their country raise their living and health standards. I can not be completely truthful, because my advice would be to practice birth control in order to have adequate food and school facilities for the population. I can not tell the people how to live, and to even go against their religion.

Since the flood in Bulacan subsided, I've been reading in the papers of the outbreak of disease there. Most of the problem is drinking water contaminated by the flood water and then the trash and mud which accumulated in the streets. Also the flies and mosquitoes are a problem. Many people there have become sick with El Tor, a form of cholera.

The mosquitoes here in Palawan are very bad. They are also the malaria carriers. I think it is fairly safe—at least I'm not going to worry until I get malaria, and then it's too late. We always sleep under a mosquito net. One morning I woke up and my arm was outside the mosquito net—oh, my! It was covered with a dozen bites.

Palawan is a beautiful island—mountainous and surrounded by water. It's located about 365 miles southwest of Manila. There is the Sulu Sea on the east and South China Sea on the west. This is quite undeveloped. The roads are very rough. It is relatively uninhabited, except right around Puerto Princesa, which is the capital.

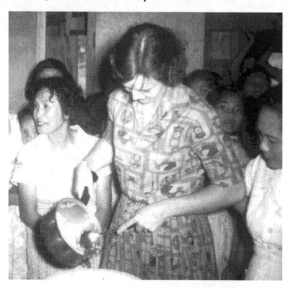

Since arriving in Palawan, I've given two foods demonstrations to a ladies' RIC, Rural Improvement Club. It's very difficult for the people to realize we don't have the same kinds of foods they do. The ladies are amazed that I don't know how to make gelatin desserts and salad from sea weed and have never heard of banana blossom soup.

I've had a delightful time planting and harvesting rice. One day we went to the Iwahig Penal Colony. In this prison there are no bars or guards, or at least none that I noticed, and the men are allowed to farm. It was here I had a chance to plant rice. I wasn't very fast, but the fellows were amazed that an American, especially a girl, would want to learn to plant and harvest rice. It was very hot and we waded in mud knee deep, but it was quite interesting and different.

Last night, again, I practiced doing the 'Tinikling'. It's a dance using bamboo poles in which the dancer jumps between bamboo poles as they are clapped to the rhythm of lively music. A fellow and I are supposed to do this dance when the Secretary of Education comes on August 17.

The tinikling is the national dance of the Philippines. The dance got its name from the tikling bird. The movements of the dance imitate the bird as the tikling bird would walk between grass stems, run over tree branches, or dodge bamboo traps set by rice farmers. The tinikling dancers replicate the bird's grace, speed, and skill, by maneuvering between bamboo poles. The poles are used as a percussion instrument, as they are moved across the ground and clapped together hard enough to make a sound. The dancers have to move quickly to avoid getting their foot or feet caught between the poles.

Love, Doris

5th Host Family Aug. 26-Sept. 15

Mr. and Mrs. Emeterio dela Cruz   Aug. 26-Sept. 15
San Mateo
Laoag, Ilocos Norte
Children: Helen, Rudy, Floro, Lena, and Napoleon

August 31, 1962
Laoag, Ilocos Norte

Dear Al,

We are again experiencing a typhoon. The irrigation canals are full, and the river is overflowing its banks. Our home is in a high area, so it is not flooded. Many bridges have been destroyed, trees blown down, and the town proper of Laoag is flooded.

Sunday, Aug. 26, I came to Ilocos Norte by plane from Manila. I'm really glad to be here before the typhoon came. I'd be afraid to fly in this kind of weather.

I am living with my 5th host family. Our home is in a barrio or rural area. My father is a farmer. He raises rice, sugar cane, garlic, onions, and corn. My host father is very much like my own dad. There are five children in the family, but only two are at home—a brother (age 22), a college graduate in agriculture; and a sister age 13. The others are away going to college.

This morning early I was awakened by something shaking my bed. When I opened my eyes I didn't see anyone or anything, so thought perhaps I was only dreaming. Later, my father told me we had a slight earthquake. My! Unusual things happen in the Philippines.

I'm living with the dela Cruz family in the northern part of the Philippines, the province of Ilocos Norte. Rudy dela Cruz, my host brother, who is about my age, is an agricultural extension agent. He is teaching me how to graft or propagate mango trees.

The people are always apologizing for their primitive living conditions, but I don't find it a hardship. I love the farm and people. Our home has no electricity, but a very good kerosene lamp. We get up early, usually 4:30 or 5:00 a.m.

My parents are protestant. This is the first protestant family I've lived with. The others have all been Catholic. I don't get much good out of going to the Catholic Church, because the service is always in Latin or Tagalog.

Last night my brother and the 4-Hers serenaded me. They came at 11:30 p.m. I was sleeping soundly. My host mother said they had sung five songs before I woke up; needless to say, it was a surprise.

The days and <u>nights</u> are always filled with surprises and many wonderful things happening.

Love, Doris

~~~~

Sept. 14, 1962
Laoag, Ilocos Norte

Dear Al,

Tomorrow I will be leaving this province for Negros Oriental. This week marks the halfway point of my stay here in the Philippines. The time is really going too fast. This host family has been one of the very nicest families I could have stayed with.

My IFYE brother, Larry, has been sick. He ate some spoiled meat, drank contaminated water, or something. I had an upset stomach only two times; and both times it was from eating too much, I think.

Please don't laugh—I've gained ten pounds. My skirts are too tight around the waist, and when Larry saw me after six weeks he said, "My gosh, you're getting fat."

I got a letter from mother last week saying that Evelyn Hoyt's father was killed in a car accident. Her mother was hurt seriously and I don't know about Evelyn. I was just wondering if Evelyn went ahead with her teaching contract at Leavenworth. This was really a shock to me because Evelyn's dad was also like a father to me. I can't help but worry about Evelyn. She was very close to her dad.

Love, Doris

We fly between islands in a small single engine plane flown by bush pilots. These planes seat one or two passengers. They also deliver mail from Manila to the more remote islands.

On the various islands, we travel by private jeep or by public transportation in jeepneys. The word jeepney is a combination of the words jeep and jitney. As World War II came to an end, there were millions of surplus army jeeps. These were either sold or given to local Filipinos. The Filipinos made them into public transportation by stripping them down to accommodate several passengers and painting them flamboyant colors with bright chrome hood ornaments. The jeepney transports not only people, but the passengers can also bring their goats, chickens, or pigs along—whatever they need to carry to market. The refurbishment of the old army jeeps into jeepneys quickly created an inexpensive means of public transportation, which had been virtually destroyed during World War II. These jeepneys had none of the modern day amenities such as air conditioning, and were notorious for smoke belching, as most of them run on diesel. As more and more Filipinos relied on jeepneys as a means of income, the government began to put restrictions on their use. Drivers were required to have specialized licenses, reasonably fixed rates, and regular routes. Jeepneys have become a symbol of the Philippine culture.

While in a jeepney, often it could be ones' misfortune to be seated beside a man or woman chewing betel nut. This is a chew similar to chewing tobacco; but produces a red juice, which the chewer usually spits out. Once I was seated by the window and the passenger chewing betel nut was seated toward the middle. He decided he needed to spit, and all of a sudden, without warning, there it went—right across in front of my face. Luckily, he was a good aim, and the juice didn't get on me or any of the other passengers. Betel nut comes from the areca nut, which grows on a palm tree in tropical areas. Chewing betel nut provides a slight stimulant similar to drinking a cup of coffee.

6th Host Family Sept. 25-Oct. 16
Mr. and Mrs. Estanislao Turtal
Tandayag Amlan, Negros Oriental
Children: Dehlia, Annie, Walter, and Opit

October 3, 1962
Dumaguete City, Negros Oriental

Dear Al,

Yes, it is still very warm here, but I'm accustomed to it now and really enjoy it. My skin has turned about three shades darker, and my hair is becoming sun bleached, so by the time I get back it may be blond.

Negros Oriental is the 5th province where I've stayed, and I am living with my 6th host family. We live only ¼ mile from the sea. Our home is a typical rural Filipino house made of nipa leaves and bamboo—very spacious and comfortable. I have two host brothers and two sisters. Besides the immediate family living in the home, there are also: grandmother, uncle and his two children, brother-in-law, grandson, and three or four maids. Labor is cheap, so everyone has a couple of maids. My father is an elementary school teacher (5th grade). The setting around our home is really beautiful. It's surrounded by coconut and banana trees—mountains to the west, north, and south, and a beach to the east.

Love, Doris

~~~~

October 10, 1962
Dumaguete, Negros Oriental

Dear Al,

It seems my stay in this province is somewhat subdued after the hectic schedule in Ilocos Norte. The first part of my stay in Dumaguete was interrupted because I was sick. For five days I chilled and ran a fever of 102. The doctor really scared me, first diagnosing it as malaria, because I'd just come from Palawan where the mosquitoes were especially bad. Later, he discovered the fever was caused by a small foot infection, as a result of a wound I hadn't had time to take care of properly. The foot injury was actually just a very small scrape, which ordinarily wouldn't have caused any problems. The hot, humid climate here causes germs to grow rapidly in situations which otherwise would amount to nothing. I didn't bother to tell my parents at home. It was only minor and they would have just worried.

I received a nice letter from Evelyn. She was hurt badly in the wreck, but was still able to arrive at her teaching job in Leavenworth. Her mother will be in the hospital until Christmas at least, and probably won't walk again for a year.

I've met several Peace Corp volunteers. They are doing a wonderful job here helping improve the schools, farm practices, and teaching homemakers new skills.

People here are very resourceful and frugal. They use all their natural plant materials to their advantage. We visited a paper factory where the paper was made from sugar cane pulp. The leftover debris from canning pineapple at the pineapple plantations such as core and peelings are fed to the livestock. Nipa palms are woven into thatch and used on roofs of rural homes. Nothing goes to waste.

Love, Doris

7th Host Family Oct. 17-Nov. 5
Dr. and Mrs. Roberto Datiles
Kabasalan, Zamboanga del Sur
Children: Larry (17), Cherry (14), Nonong (11), and Chelo (10)

I am in Mindanao now, the southern-most island of the Philippines. I'm staying with a wonderful family. My father is a physician and was in the United States for 3 years. Mother was there one year. They are so much like Americans; sometimes I forget where I am. There are four children in the family—Larry (17) studying Commerce in Manila 2nd year, Cherry (14), Nonong (11), and Chelo (10).

The work of a doctor is really hard in the Philippines. The second night I was here, my host father let me watch while he delivered a baby. The equipment is primitive, but I admired his skill.

The town of Kabasalan is still quite undeveloped, but nowhere in the world can you find nicer, friendlier people. They are wonderful.

Kabasalan, Zamboanga del Sur
October 17, 1962
Wednesday

Dear Al,

Today I had a short visit with IFYE brother, Larry. Then I met with Miss Malicsi and two other extension workers, who took me from Dipolog to Kabasalan, Zamboanga del Sur. At Kabasalan I will be living with my 7th host family. The trip was about 480 kilometers. We traveled by jeep over bumpy, unpaved roads. The ride was hot and dusty, but I enjoyed the trip in spite of this. The scenery was spectacular. During most of the trip, we drove along the beach through mountainous country. The trip took eight hours. We left Dipolog at 10:30 a.m., and arrived in Kabasalan at 6:30 p.m. I was really tired.

Love, Doris

~~~~

October 18, 1962
Thursday

This morning we visited the town proper of Kabasalan and went to my host father's farm. At the farm we planted banana suckers and ate coconut.

In the afternoon, it rained very hard. My brothers and sisters didn't have to go to school today, so we played games this afternoon. Mother and Cherry taught me to play mahjong.

Tonight we made a chocolate cake. Cherry, Mother, Chelo, and I worked together to make it; although the boys were always nearby watching and were interested. I really enjoyed helping cook, and the family appreciated the cake.

Oct. 19, 1962

Tonight, for the first time since I left home, almost six months ago, I tasted mashed potatoes. This family really knows what kind of food Americans eat. They also have milk, apples, pancakes, and oranges—a rarity here.

Oct. 20, 1962
Saturday

This morning I went with my family to Hercules Lumber Camp, which is about 19 kilometers from Kabasalan, where my host father goes once a week to doctor the men and families at the lumber camp.

Later we attended a barrio fiesta at crossing Santa Clara. We visited two houses and ate plenty at each. We also followed the custom of "bring house", where the visiting family is also urged to take some food home. Larry, Cherry, Chelo, Nonong, and I, observed a cockfight.

Chelo has a yellow tiger cat, which she calls Sultan. He is really a pet. Yesterday, she even painted his toenails with finger nail polish.

The children love each other, but still have their little disagreements—unlike my other host families where the children seemed to get along so unnaturally well. Here the boys tease and mimic the girls just like my brothers, Loyde and Ray—just to aggravate their sisters.

October 22, 1962

This was a very big and exciting day. My host family and I were invited to the home of Capt. and Mrs. Pedro Changco, who have a huge rubber plantation.

October 24, 1962

This morning I visited the elementary school of Kabasalan where Chelo is in grade 4. I am always warmed and honored by the wonderful welcome I receive everywhere. The children and teachers had prepared a fabulous welcome program. I talked to about 300 students. The home economics students, grades 5 and 6, prepared homemade ice cream. Was it ever delicious. I ate three cups full.

I rested this afternoon. I was really worn out. Sometimes the terrific heat makes me feel sleepy and sluggish.

October 25, 1962

This morning we visited Mindanao and Zamboanga Rubber Company. Between the two plantations, they have 2,000 hectares, 4,500 acres, of rubber trees. We went to the home of Mr. and Mrs. Jose Changco—really a wonderful couple.

Around noon, we went to the Naga fishing village. There we saw fishermen bringing in their catch. I saw how fish are dried under the sun. The entire village had an acrid odor, but I suppose the families there get used to it.

It's really amazing how the little children come running to look at the 'Americano'. One child sees me and sends out a message, I believe; anyway, very soon about a million little kids come running to see. They stand staring and smiling with their big brown eyes shining. They always follow along and try to get as close as they can. Filipino children are <u>very</u> shy, but I love them.

Fish Drying on Slatted Frames

This afternoon, I went to the Kabasalan High School. I sang and taught them a square dance. They learned fast and were really delighted. I thoroughly enjoyed teaching them, too. During the square dance, the students were even shouting with enthusiasm. They were a wonderfully receptive group.

Later, the home economics girls served refreshments. I had been eating all day, and they had prepared so much. The teachers were all bringing me food, and I was already full (busog). When no teachers or extension people were watching, I slyly gave the food to some of the little children who were staring at me.

October 26, 1962
Friday

This was a very interesting and educational day. Very early this morning, we prepared to attend a Muslim mass. We dressed as Muslims and were accompanied by a Muslim, Mr. Habib. The mass was held in a barrio called Mamagon. In order to get there, we went in an outboard banca for about 30 minutes. Part of the ride was at sea. Also, at Mamagon we attended a Farmer's Extension Club graduation. I was asked to speak to about 40 Muslim farmers.

The Muslim mass was quite unusual. First, the men and women wash themselves (face, arms, ears, and feet) before entering the chapel. The men change from their pants to malong, a long piece of cloth wrapped around them. They believe that they should not worship in their dirty work clothes. Their mass is very short, 20-30 minutes, with much kneeling, murmuring, and motioning. During the mass, the men kneel at the front of the church facing the rising sun, and the women kneel at the rear.

After a big day, we returned by banca. When we reached Kabasalan, we rode in an ox cart to our house. What a fabulous experience. I thoroughly enjoyed it. The children remarked, "Americano Mora" meaning American Muslim, because I was dressed like a Muslim.

I'll describe what a banca is like. Since the Philippines have over 7,000 islands, there is an incredible amount of shore line. It is easy to estimate that over half the country's population live at or near the beach. Bancas are a means of navigating the seas and waterways of the Philippines. Typically, a banca is a hand carved canoe used to transport the fisherman's catch, cargo, or family members. This mode of transportation has been in use for hundreds of years. The early bancas were relatively unstable and would easily tip over, especially if someone stood up in them. Over time, out-riggers were added to each side of the banca for stability. Today the banca is still in use, but has evolved into a much lighter weight model made from wood readily available in the Philippines. Most of them are mobilized by paddling, but some are motorized.

Oct. 29, 1962

Today we went to Ipil, Zamboanga del Sur. I met the mayor of Ipil, Mayor Sukgang. He married a mestiza, Filipina/American. His wife is the daughter of old man Donton, an American, who came here long ago and married many wives—five to be exact.

Tonight the people of Ipil had a welcome dance in honor of my coming. This was the first time for me to see "Benny Boys", who are men dressed and acting as women. They actually had on high heels and were dancing with men. I enjoyed the dance and was requested to dance the twist and sing.

I'll be leaving this province Nov. 7th. From here I'll go to Iligan City, which is also in Mindanao, the province of Lanao del Norte. There are Muslims here. We had a chance to attend their mass yesterday.

I'm going to spend Halloween with a middle aged American couple, Mr. and Mrs. Komaromi, who have been here 15 years with Goodyear Rubber Company. They have a beautiful mansion on top of a hill overlooking the plantation. There are many large rubber plantations in this province.

Goodyear plantation has approximately 1500 hectares of rubber trees. The plantation was started in 1929. I've had a chance to see how rubber trees are tapped. There is good money in raising rubber trees, and the land here is almost free.

The Komaromi's house is beautiful, and their yard is spectacular. All the bedrooms are air conditioned, and they have at least 3 beautiful bathrooms. My bedroom was like a dream. I didn't have to sleep under a mosquito net tonight. It was wonderful for a change.

Tonight, the Schneider's, assistant manager of Goodyear, came up. We had a good old fashioned American picnic in the

Philippines: baked beans, potato salad, hot dogs, hamburgers, and pumpkin pie. They even had a Jack-o'-lantern!

Nov. 2, 1962

I returned home to my Datiles family this morning. I was glad to be back. When asked by my host father how my stay was at Goodyear, I replied, "I had a wonderful time, but I'm glad to be home". He beamed.

This afternoon, we visited the Santa Clara plywood factory. It was really interesting to observe the many processes of making plywood. They are exporting plywood to the U.S. Mr. Zagala is the manager there.

We got into an absolute downpour going to Santa Clara. Dad and I both got soaked, because we were seated near the outside of the jeep.

November 5, 1962

Today Miss Malicsi the extension worker and I took the Zamtranco bus from Kabasalan to Zamboanga. It was a long, hot, bumpy, dirty trip. We left Kabasalan at 6:30 a.m., and arrived in Zamboanga at 3:00 p.m.

Tonight, Miss Malicsi and I are sleeping in the 'Tree House' at Pasonanca Park. It is a fabulous tree house complete with bathroom, refrigerator, stove, and everything, including sleeping accommodations for two. What fun! It has all the amenities of a small motel room. Guests can stay there free of charge after getting permission from the mayor.

At the base of the Pasonanca tree house is this poem.

I think that I shall not see
A poem lovely as a tree
A tree that looks at God all day
And lifts her leafy arms to pray.
A tree that may in summer wear
A nest of robins in her hair;
Upon whose bosom snow has lain,
Who intimately lives with rain
Poems are made by fools like me,
But only God can make a tree.

By Joyce Kilmer

November 7, 1962

We took a small single engine plane, called an Otter, from Zamboanga City to Pagadian. The ride was enjoyable, but very noisy. My long legs, and the Filipino size seats in the plane, had a conflict.

November 8, 1962

I'm staying a couple of days in the home of Mr. Pescador, the provincial agriculturalist of Zamboanga del Sur. I've been moving around so much, I hardly have any clean clothes left. This is the fourth day of wearing the same dress, and it's beginning to smell. The Filipinos have often said, "You Americans wear your clothes out washing them." That's certainly not the case with this dress.

November 9, 1962

Traveled from Pagadian this morning to Lala, Lanao del Norte to stay with my last host family, Mr. and Mrs. Lim and their children.

8th Host Family Nov. 9-22
Mr. and Mrs. Glicerio A. Lim   Lanipao, Lala, Lanao del Norte
Children: Ben, Nicholas, Susan, Allan, Joy, Aurora, and Jr.

This host father is a banker, but they also have a farm. Right now they're in the midst of rice harvest. In this area, corn and rice are the primary crops. Farmers raise three crops of corn and two of rice a year.

Lim Family

I had a fabulous day. I went with my host brother, Ben to the farm. I watched while the provincial agriculturalist castrated a carabao. That was very interesting. Ben let me try my luck at plowing with a hand plow and carabao. It's really much harder than it looks. I had a terrible time getting the carabao to go where I wanted him to. Ben has a Fordson tractor, which we used to ride to the farm. I got to see one of the few examples of mechanized farming in the Philippines. He farms about 48 hectares (100 acres).

Later Ben and I went to the elementary school where my youngest host brother, Allan, is in the 6th grade. While there I taught some of the teachers the Virginia Reel, we danced the Tango, and I planted a mangosteen tree in the school yard.

That afternoon, I sang to Lillibeth, 3 years old, until she went to sleep. I love her very much. She's such a darling little girl.

In a Christmas card written December 14, 1964 my host father Lim writes:

May the blessings of the Christmas season bring you lasting happiness and prosperity in the New Year. The whole family is well. To remember you, we have named the daughter of Aurora, 'Doris Marie'. She was born on March 14, 1963.

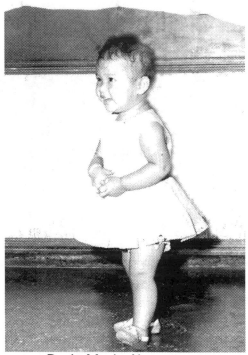

Doris Marie Aleucay

Lillibeth is fine and will enroll in kindergarten next June.

Ben is doing well. He is with the Philippine Tobacco Administration promoting the tobacco industry in our locality to export.

The mangosteen tree that you planted is growing fine. There was a new building erected near it, but they were careful not to damage the tree. I will try to take a picture of it and send it to you.

We all send our love and best wishes to you and Alvin.

Father and Mother Lim

Foods

The durian fruit is a delicacy and favorite among the Filipino people. It is a large fruit, which has a tough thorny husk on the outside, with delicious rich, buttery-smooth flesh on the inside. However, durian has a disagreeable odor, which turns most people off. It is often described as "the fruit that smells like hell, but tastes like heaven." While almost everyone who tastes the durian fruit agrees the taste is heavenly, no two ever describe the taste the same.

Since the Philippines is a warm and temperate climate, many delicious fruits and vegetables flourish, and are available year round. Some of the fruits are papaya, pineapple, rambutan, santol, star fruit, tambis, guava, jackfruit, lemonsito, mango, mangosteen, atis, banana, and coconut.

With one whack of a Filipino's bolo knife, a coconut can be cut open. The coconut milk is poured into a glass; fresh grated coconut and sugar are added for a delicious treat. This is very refreshing on a hot afternoon.

Local farmers often set up fire pits along the roadside where they sell corn on the cob roasted in the husk. It is really juicy and tasty.

Doris and Larry in a Pineapple Field

During the last few days of November, I stayed with Mr. and Mrs. Fred Santiago in Cagayan de Oro. Mr. Santiago is a Provincial Home Demonstrator, who works for the Del Monte Packing Company. November 29th we visited the Del Monte pineapple plantation. It was really interesting and amazing to see acre after acre of pineapple plants growing. There were 80,000 hectares. 1 hectare = about 2.5 acres, so there were 200,000 acres of pineapples on the Del Monte plantation. We were given eight fresh pineapples—huge ones, very juicy and sweet. The plantation was managed by United States men, who were living there with their families.

Lanao del Norte
Nov. 14, 1962

Dear Al,

I'm living with my last host family on Lanao del Norte. I really like it here, because they let me help on the farm by trying to plow and gather eggs.

I've received word from D.C. regarding our trip home. We will be leaving here Dec. 9. We will have only 5 days in Europe, Jan. 4-9. Then will arrive in New York Jan. 18. Our final consultation program in Washington D.C. will be from Jan. 19-23. I think I will fly home Jan. 23 or 24.

My stay in the Philippines has been tremendous, but I am anxious to get home and start working—and also lead a relatively normal life again. Here I'm always in the public eye—giving speeches and going to parties.

I'm having a good time learning some Filipino songs. The words are really hard, but the people are so pleased to hear an American sing their songs.

Love, Doris

Plowing Rice Paddies Using Carabao

Doris Gives Plowing a Try

November 22, 1962

Left Lala, Lanao del Norte and arrived at Marawi City, Lanao del Norte

November 22-23, 1962

I'm staying two days in the home of Gov. Alonto, a Muslim.

November 24, 1962

Left Marawi City for Iligan

Nov. 24-26, 1962

Host family Mr. and Mrs. Jose Gaudiongco
Children: Erlinda—16, Folilin—13, and Reynaldo—18.

I left by bus about 8 a.m. for Iligan City. I arrived at the home of Mr. and Mrs. Jose Gaudiongco, who is the office manager at the PAL, Philippine Air Line. I feel my stay here is too short. This family is very interested in the IFYE program, and in the United States. My sister, Erlinda, is only 16 years old, but is very smart. The family is building a new home. Soon, they will be moving into it. They can't move in during December. There is a superstition, that if you move into a new home the last month of the year that it's bad luck.

November 27-30, 1962

Traveled from Iligan to Cagayan de Oro. I'm staying with Mr. and Mrs. Fred Santiago. They have five children, all girls. They are very sweet and pretty little girls. Fred works for Del Monte Packing Company. We visited the Del Monte Packing Company and Del Monte pineapple plantation.

November 30, 1962

Left Cagayan de Oro for Manila. I flew from Cagayan de Oro to Manila. It was sad to realize I was leaving Mindanao for good.

December 1-7, 1962
Manila

Larry and I spent one hectic, frustrating, fabulous, and <u>tiring</u> final week in Manila. Our days began at 5:30 a.m., and ended no earlier than 12 midnight (sometimes 1:30 or 3 a.m.). I don't know how we lasted. We went all-day sightseeing, saying 'good-byes' to USIS, Embassy, AIO, and many others. In the evening, we were invited to parties and dinner. It was a grand finale to a wonderful experience.

Excerpts taken from a post card
Aboard the ship S.S. Vietnam

Dec. 10, 1962

Dear Al,

We flew PAL, Philippine Air Lines, from Manila to Hong Kong. We left Hong Kong last night at 12 midnight. We boarded a ship called the S.S. Vietnam headed for Singapore. This was the first time in five months I've had a <u>hot</u> shower. It was really a luxury. We'll be arriving in New York January 18th.

~~~~

From a letter written to Al Johnson from Singapore

Singapore
December 17, 1962

Dear Al,

We docked in Singapore this morning and will be leaving tonight in a few hours, so I wanted to write in hopes you'll receive this before Christmas. Our next port is Colombo on Dec. 21.
We went to the Wesley Methodist Church this morning. It's a very beautiful church and the first time I'd attended a

Methodist service since early June.   The sermon was in English.

I am really anxious to be home. It was sad leaving the Philippines, but now I am between my two beloved countries and feel like a man without a country or home. This is rather an empty feeling, especially at Christmas time. It's very warm and doesn't feel at all like the middle of December.

We have only five days in Europe.   Our ship reaches Marseille, France on January 4th. We depart on January 9th from LeHavre for the last leg of our voyage. While traveling across France, we plan to rent a car.   That should be very interesting since none of us speak French.

I'll bet you and your students are all ready for a nice long Christmas vacation. It must be hard to teach and keep their attention just before a vacation.

Love, Doris

~~~~

Excerpt from post card written from
Colombo, Ceylon
Dec. 19, 1962

Deal Al,

We are a long way from anything, but lots of water. This is the 9th day on the ship and it's beginning to get to me. Much more of this and I'll start swimming ashore. Guess you might say, I'm a little anxious to get home.

Doris

~~~~

Post card written from Bombay, India
Dec. 22, 1962

Dear Al,

I was delighted to receive your Christmas card when we docked in Ceylon. You are certainly worried about my teeth!

Just like a doting mother. Yes, I brushed my teeth regularly in water. I never did drink boiled water and was only sick twice from impure water. There were all sorts of alcoholic drinks made from coconut juice, sugar cane sap, rice, and about everything else.

Love, Doris

~~~~

Aboard the S. S. Vietnam
Nearing Marseille, France
January 2, 1963

Dear Al,

We are crossing the Mediterranean Sea now and will be arriving at Marseille, France on Janurary 5th. Our ship was delayed one day getting through the Suez Canal, which means we'll have only four days in Europe. We plan to go to LeHavre, stopping only one day in Paris for sightseeing and shopping. The four of us are going to rent a car.

Day before yesterday, Dec. 31, we spent the day in Cairo, Egypt. It was really fabulous. We saw the pyramids, sphinx, museum, several mosques, and had a camel ride. The camel ride was great. I'm still stiff today. Do you know they even have saddles for the camels?

We actually got to go inside one of the pyramids. This was accomplished by crawling on our hands and knees through a long, narrow tunnel until we reached the center of the pyramid. Once inside, we were able to stand up in a room that held a stone casket in which one of Egypt's pharaohs was buried.

The pyramids are huge limestone rocks layered to form the pyramid shape. They were built hundreds of years ago. The work was done over a period of 80 years by 20,000-30,000 people. The huge limestone boulders were believed to have been floated down the flooded Nile River, and rolled by the use of primitive tools to the area where the pyramids now stand.

The Sphinx is a stone statue near the pyramids that has the body of a lion and head of a human. It is also hundreds of years old and very large. Every year thousands of tourists go to see the pyramids and Sphinx.

It is beginning to get very cold, and today as we passed some land we saw snow capped mountains. It reminded me of the beloved Rockies.

I haven't heard from the folks since I left Manila. I just realized we have been on this ship almost a month. It's no wonder we're looking forward to getting off in Marseille.

December 31 was a big day. We got up at 5:30 a.m. to go to Cairo. That night we got stranded from our ship, because it had trouble getting through the Suez Canal, so our group spent New Years Eve in a dumpy hotel in Port Said. We didn't get to the hotel until 1:30 a.m., January 1st. We were all nearly frozen stiff. We were too cold to sleep, so Larry and I stayed up until 4 a.m. talking. We finally went to bed and were up again at 7 a.m. to catch our ship.

I'll try to write again before we leave LeHavre.

Love, Doris

Larry and Doris Riding Camels

Atlantic Ocean aboard the S.S. Ryndam, of the Holland American Line.
January 11, 1963

Dear Al,

I received your letter in Djibouti. It was really nice to get some mail again.

We reached Marseille, France on January 5, rented a car and set out for Paris. We all had a grand time. It was very cold. I even drove a little, and driving in France is quite a trick, believe me. The boys nearly had a heart attack. My driver's license was expired, so if we'd been caught, it would have been just too bad.

To save money, we ate French bread and cheese for three days and a few other ridiculous things. We weren't really trying to economize, but just couldn't find a place to get our money changed, since it was the weekend.

The Ryndam is a fabulous ship. It is part of the Holland-American fleet of passenger ships. It seems like a castle—maybe because it's taking us to good ole USA. The ocean is quite rough. Many people are seasick, and last night I didn't feel so well either. Everything on the ship is very convenient—even for seasickness—at very strategic places they have placed "barf bags".

Sharon, IFYE to Taiwan, and I have one of the lower cabins with a porthole. The waves really splash up high—15 to 20 feet and cover our window. Sometimes it bangs so loud you think the whole ocean is coming right in. The ship is beautiful inside and well equipped. There is a library, movie every day, organ music, trio, and dancing. There are about 200 college students on here. It's one big ball all the time.

You would have a good time on this ship. Some of the people speak German. Our dining room steward speaks English and German. I have a good time saying a few words to him in German.

You asked how we send and receive mail from a ship— well, whenever the ship stops at a port the passengers can go ashore. We can find a post office and mail letters ourselves, or a member of the ship's crew will mail letters for us. It's really very simple.

See you soon.
Love, Doris

~~~~

After arriving back home in Brewster, Kansas this was a newspaper article that appeared in the *Sherman County Herald* on February 7, 1963.

Busy Speaking Schedule Ahead For IFYE Student
By *Virginia Lee Mathews*

A busy speaking schedule in the next two months really won't be too hard for Doris Imhof to handle, since she has become accustomed to giving speeches and keeping busy during the six month stay in the Philippines.

Doris, who was in the Philippines, as an International Farm Youth Exchange student, arrived home a week ago; and already has 18 speaking engagements for February and March.

The tall brunette from Brewster said that she first realized she was home in New York City when the taxi driver understood English, and "I didn't have to try and make him understand where I wanted to go."

She added that she did not have too much trouble getting around in the Philippines, because the extension service people usually took her. The thing that bothered her most about the language was word pronunciation when trying to speak their native language. Most Filipinos spoke English. Their national language is Tagalog.

One of my host fathers had been to the United States and was trying to tell me about the 'pecken' trees. Finally, I understood he meant 'pecan' trees.

Helped in the Fields

Busy from dawn to dusk, Doris helped with the housework, yard and field work, and gave speeches.

Tasks on an average day for Filipino families included doing the laundry by hand, sweeping, dusting, cooking, raking leaves, planting trees, napping, eating five times a day, and helping in the fields.

"I didn't have too much trouble cooking," Doris said. "They don't have the same kind of ingredients or spices that we have and no baking powder because it's hard to get. They do have small potatoes, but don't use potatoes much in their cooking."

"Chicken, pork, and lots of fish, as well as fresh fruits and vegetables, make up the diet. They eat very little beef."

One host father let Doris try her hand at plowing—with a walking plow.

Carabao Plow Power

"I helped plow once, but I wasn't a great success. I couldn't do it for long periods of time because my arms tired easily. The furrow was too shallow, too." She laughed and added, "They told me plowing didn't really take strength, and I guess it doesn't because a young boy can do it."

Similar to the oxen once used in the United States, a carabao pulls the plow. Doris said that even though her plowing career did not last long, she liked to ride the animal.

Since the purpose of her stay in the Philippines as an International Farm Youth Exchange delegate was to promote better understanding, she gave talks to 4-H groups and schools on 4-H club work in the United States, her home and family, and what farming is like in western Kansas.

Embarrassing Questions

She also answered questions about the differences in the school systems, the Cuban Crisis, and the African-American situation as well as she could.

"I was rather embarrassed when a Filipino asked me if he would be treated like James Meredith if he came to this country. The people just couldn't understand how a democracy could treat its' people that way."

James Meredith, an American civil rights activist, was the first African-American student to be admitted to the University of Mississippi. He became a student there in 1962, but is was not without rioting and blood shed. Two people were killed and many others injured in the rioting.

"Anything that happens to the United States, the Filipinos feel happens to them, too," Doris said, "so naturally, they were worried about the Cuban situation, also."

In reference to schooling, Doris pointed out that students in the islands are only required to complete grade six. She added that high school followed the sixth grade and that students are attending college at 15 or 16.

"With students going to college young, I expected a well equipped educational system," she said. "But, text books are badly needed. Organizations in the United States send used books for school use."

Lots of Rain

The outstanding things Doris remembers about the Philippines are the country's "friendly people and rain."

"At first the heat and dampness bothered me," Doris said, "but after I got used to it, I liked not having to wear a coat."

Coats are not worn even when it rained because they really "were not much good" and the "sun comes out soon to dry you out."

Filipinos are so friendly, that Doris had to learn not to brag about their food or praise their belongings, because she would immediately receive the item or items as a gift. She can not remember the number of boxes which she shipped from the Philippines, but so far sixteen of them have arrived in Brewster.

Jars of Jelly

When she visited one family's home for the afternoon and commented on the mangosteen jelly, she immediately received several jars of it. Some of them lasted long enough to come back to the United States. Other gifts include pineapple fiber handkerchiefs, bamboo fans, a formal dress, Filipino house dress, and items carved of wood. The typical dress of the Filipino housewife is a red plaid jumper with a pineapple fiber over-blouse. The outfit is called a balintawak.

Other very unique gifts were jewelry made of ipil ipil seeds (seeds looking very much like apple seeds) from the acacia tree. Ipil ipil trees can be found anywhere in the Philippines, but Palawan is a key area where cultural production using these seeds occurs today. The ipil ipil tree is used to control erosion. The seeds are known to have medicinal properties as well. The young seeds are green in color. The mature seeds, when dried turn brown and are being made into bags, bracelets, necklaces, and other jewelry. Ipil ipil trees can be found in urban and rural areas in the Philippines.

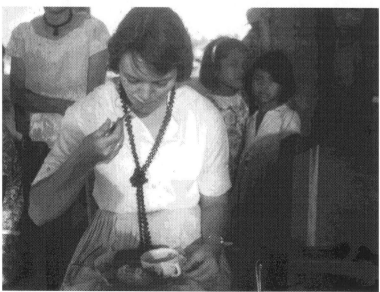

Doris Wearing Ipil Seed Necklace

Perhaps the greatest gift of all was having a child named after her brother, Ray Dean. She said her host father in one province named his baby boy after her brother. Doris' family received pictures of the family and baby the following Christmas.

Ray Dean and Arlene Paredes

Doris has a younger sister, Carol, a senior in high school, and another brother, Loyde, who is married and lives in Colby. The whole family is very proud of her, but her mother, Mrs. Robert Imhof, said, "I don't know where we will put all the other boxes when they arrive."

Looking forward to being an extension agent, Doris who graduated from Kansas State University, is glad to be home and thrilled with her experiences.

~~~~

Impressions Filipino People Have Of Americans

Every morning and night I help my host mother feed the hogs and gather eggs. They think it's unusual to see an American doing work like this. It's their impression that all Americans are rich and don't have to work. They acquired these misconceptions from movies and television.

Bayanihan Dance Troupe

As a way of preserving part of the Philippine culture, the Bayanihan Dance Troupe was formed in 1956. Since it was founded, the dance troupe strives to research and preserve indigenous Philippine art forms in music, dance, costumes, and folklore. The dance performances are seen as a way to promote international goodwill in the Philippines and around the world. This talented dance troupe has performed in countless countries and cities all over the world, much to the entertainment and delight of their audiences. The Philippine government officially declared the Bayanihan Philippine Dance Troupe as The Philippine National Folk Dance Troupe.

A Different Way of Life

It was really a different experience to wash clothes in the river by beating them on the rocks. Sometimes the water is so dirty, I don't know how the clothes ever get clean. Then the wet clothes are laid on the grass to dry.

People are really carefree here. They are only concerned with the things necessary for survival. They're not very concerned about the past or the future. They live in the present.

Because the climate in the Philippines is so hot and humid, the people lead a much slower-paced life than ours in the United States. In the afternoon during the hottest part of the day, families and workers take a siesta for 1-2 hours when they rest or sleep. They also laughed about their 'Filipino Time'. This is what they called it when people were typically anywhere from thirty minutes to two hours late arriving at and starting meetings. This was common-place and nobody seemed to be bothered by it.

They'd just show up when they got 'good and ready'. Maybe Americans should be a little more like that. There would be a lot fewer cases of ulcers and high blood pressure.

Laundry Day at the River

On Dec. 9, 1962, we boarded a plane from Manila to Hong Kong to begin our journey home. In Hong Kong we boarded the ship, S.S. Vietnam. The port stops we made along the way back to the United States were: Singapore, Colombo, Djibouti, Bombay, Cairo, the Suez Canal, Marseille, and Le Havre. We spent Christmas day basking in the sun on the deck of the ship in the middle of the Mediterranean Sea. At Marseille we rented a car and drove across France. Along the way we stopped and spent time in Paris. At Le Havre our tiny group of 4 boarded a ship for the pilgrimage across the Atlantic Ocean. Our destination was New York City. By now it was mid-winter, and the Atlantic Ocean was very choppy. The trip was turbulent, and many became seasick. We arrived in New York City Jan 18, 1963 almost 6 weeks after departing from the Philippines.

The desire to learn about other countries, their people, and cultures didn't end with my IFYE experience in 1962. I continued to be interested in world affairs and creating better understanding between countries. In 1967 Napoleon delaCruz, a host brother from the Philippines, was an IFYE to the United

States and stayed in Kansas with my family for three weeks. By 1985 the LABO program, an exchange program with Japan for 4-H youth, was growing in popularity. Our daughter, Sara, then 14 years old, and several other youth from Marysville, Kansas, spent four weeks in Japan as exchangees. The following year, I served as the local coordinator in Marysville who placed the Japanese students, who came to Kansas, with local host families. That summer we hosted a LABO girl in our home. In 2011 I met a wonderful young lady, IFYE from Sweden. Her name is Emma Hedin. I had the opportunity and pleasure of inviting her to my home and showing her around historic Abilene, Kansas.

1998 found me going abroad again. I spent a month in Japan as a recipient of the Fulbright Teacher Award. While there, we visited schools, interacted with students, and learned about Japan's educational system. The Japanese educators were eager to learn about United States' teaching strategies. Japan's main focus, at that time, was to combat bullying in their schools.

In 2000 my husband and I were looking for excitement and an adventure, so we signed up for a program called Bridges for Education. This group primarily consisted of teachers who would teach conversational English to high school students in Belarus. We traveled to Belarus with a small group of teachers from throughout the United States. We worked with the students headquartered at an orphanage in Smorgon, Belarus. The housing and food were primitive, but the students made up for the living conditions. We lived, ate, and did all activities with about sixty high school students from Russia, Belarus, and Poland. The students were absolutely immersed in speaking and learning the English language. It was one of the most rewarding experiences of my life. They were so eager to learn and so much fun.

My husband and I traveled throughout Germany in 2000 and again in 2005. Both times we tried to travel the back roads as much as possible by staying in the 'guest haus', eating in small cafes, and mingling with the people in the countryside. My husband has relatives there, and we spent some time with them, giving us a glimpse of how rural German people live. We rented a car which allowed us to get off the beaten path, as well as, travel the autobahn. In 2000 we did not rent a car, but rode the train from Frankfurt to Osnabruck. It was relaxing to ride along and view mile after mile of vineyards along the Rhine and the many old castles nestled high on the hillsides.

Today my greatest reward would be to travel around the world learning about other people, their way of life, foods, customs, and hoping to spread a little bit of goodwill, peace, and understanding among nations.

Epilogue

You may have wondered what life was like for each of the IFYEs as they returned from their Far East experience. I asked each delegate to write about the journey of their life and career. This is what they had to say.

Beverly Ann Malnar Morin
IFYE to Japan
From Ewen, Michigan

Following my IFYE experience in 1962, Len, my husband of forty-nine years and I have been living in Phoenix, Arizona for the last forty-four years. We were married four months after I returned to my home state of Michigan. At the time of our marriage, Len was employed in Boise, Idaho. A short time later we moved to Eugene, Oregon, where I taught second grade for two years. Another job transfer brought us to Portland, Oregon. It was in 1967 that we adopted a beautiful, loveable three month old little girl and named her Christina. I was a stay-at-home Mom for a couple of years. Later we moved to Phoenix where I taught in an elementary school of twenty-five years and retired in 1994. In 1996 we lost our twenty-six year old, unmarried daughter due to a car accident. It was a very difficult time for us.

Since that time we have kept busy doing some traveling, attending Phoenix Suns basketball games and spending our summers at Munds Park, which is just south of Flagstaff, Arizona. We're enjoying retirement.

By Bev Morin, who resides in Phoenix. Arizona.

Don Eugene Miller
IFYE to Japan
From Lowden, Washington

After returning from the IFYE trip in December 1962, Don was drafted into the Army in 1963 and served until 1969. When his tour of duty was over, he moved to Yakima and enrolled in the nursing program at Yakima Valley Community College. There he met his wife, Gerri, who was also in the nursing program. They graduated and were married in 1975.

Gerri had two young daughters, Tammy and Becky. Don adopted these little girls and they called him "Daddy Don". Their family was complete when Don and Gerri had a daughter, Sarah, and adopted another daughter, Jolene. He was not only good at the "Daddy" role, but took on "Mom" duties as well, like cooking, cleaning, sewing dresses, and fixing the girls' hair. There was nothing Don couldn't do because can't was not in his vocabulary. He raised his girls to be strong women and he was very proud of his family.

In 1986, Don moved his family to Arizona where he and Gerri attended Grand Canyon University, receiving their Bachelors in Nursing in 1989. After their graduation, the family returned to Yakima where Don served the community for twenty years as a registered nurse. Don was very caring and compassionate for his patients.

Don and Gerri traveled extensively in their motor home. They also made several trips to Hawaii throughout the years. Time spent with his girls, their husbands, and his grandchildren were life's highlights for him. He was an "extraordinary man".

We were saddened to learn of Don's death. He passed away November 14, 2009 after a courageous battle with cancer. He and Gerri were married thirty-four years.

85

Larry K. Hiller
IFYE to the Philippines
From Morning Sun, Iowa

Impact of IFYE

There is absolutely no question that the 4-H IFYE program and experience was the most important turning point in my life for several reasons. I had grown up on a general crop and livestock farm in southeastern Iowa. In both 4-H and FFA I had the opportunity for many different kinds of projects and leadership experiences. When I headed off to college at Iowa State University, I had my career vision directed towards becoming a County Extension Director or a Vocational Ag teacher in the high schools. Because of these career goals, and the fact that I was equally interested in livestock and crops, a natural choice was to major in Ag Education.

College classes were very exciting, stimulating, and challenging. Satisfaction resulted from seeing some of the changes I implemented with my father on our home farm. Additionally I enjoyed a very rewarding County Extension Trainee experience between my junior and senior years, and a less than favorable student teaching experience my senior year. Nevertheless, I was still quite confused as to what career I really wanted to pursue. Then along came the IFYE opportunity in the Philippines in 1962! I delayed graduation until after the IFYE trip as a "delay tactic" in needing to choose my first job. In retrospect that was the perfect decision because of the impact that the 8 months as an IFYE had on me. What an eye-opening experience for this Iowa farm boy who liked to joke that Minnesota was a "foreign country" to him.

I thought that I was always comfortable with all kinds of people, but exposure to people of different cultures, customs, and traditions, the opportunities to experience new life styles, foods and beliefs, religious and family values, all had an immediate impact on me. This was often confusing and not easily understood at that time, but certainly not ever in a threatening manner. But add to this the many challenges and opportunities for growth plus broadening one's perspectives, the total result was life-changing avenues for me personally and professionally.

Personally, IFYE gave me the 'travel bug' and desire to explore other countries and cultures, taught me to try almost any kind of new food or drink, listen to and be sensitive to other cultural standards, traditions, values, etc. Perhaps more importantly in many ways, it opened my eyes to the tremendous importance and value of vegetables in the human diet and nutrition. This helped direct my goals toward a career in horticulture, quite specifically vegetable crops.

The next opportunity I had, quite clearly a direct result of the IFYE experience just completed, was to be invited by the Iowa State University Dean of Agriculture, Floyd Andre, to participate in the Iowa State/USAID (Agency for International Development) "Alliance for Progress "program in Uruguay, South America. My assignment was to work with a system of 13 general and 6 specialized vocational agricultural secondary schools to help improve their teaching programs and practical skills training. Additional effort was to help develop a specialized school for vegetables and assist the University of Uruguay with their horticultural curriculum.

During the 18 months prior to actually going on this program, I finished my BS degree, got married, and completed a MS program in Horticulture, as well as began learning Spanish. The four years on the ISU/USAID program definitely solidified my desire to continue my study of vegetable crops, work towards a PhD degree, and possibly teach at the college level. Following a very productive and enriching experience in Uruguay, I was accepted into the Department of Vegetable Crops program at Cornell University. My major professor and associated Graduate Assistantship provided me the unique experiences of teaching my first college classes and serving as a mentor to all of his international students. One specific course provided the opportunity to study tropical vegetables in Jamaica. My studies and research prepared me for a fantastic career in vegetable and potato teaching/research at Washington State University, which lasted for over 35 years.

During this time I had wonderful opportunities that were strengthened because of my IFYE experience. This included being able to incorporate the international flavor into my classes and advising students, the opportunity to work with potato producers and industry all over the US and other countries, serve as a Spanish interviewer for the Latin American Scientific Program at American Universities, consultation assignments with Rockefeller Foundation in Ecuador and Peru, other programs in South Africa and Scotland, a member of Class I of the WK Kellogg National Fellows program for 3 years, and a truly rewarding 3 week experience in Russia with my father advising on farm cooperatives.

Obviously, the IFYE program and experience had a major impact on my personal and professional life for 50 years. This has constantly been important during all those years and even more so now in our "smaller" world and increased interactions in our everyday lives. Certainly deeply engrained in my beliefs and actions are the IFYE theme song "This Is My Song" ["A Song of Peace"] and IFYE motto "World Peace through Understanding."

Written by Larry Hiller, who resides in Pullman, Washington.

Doris Imhof Johnson
IFYE to the Philippines
From Brewster, Kansas

Shortly after returning from the Philippines I was hired in Graham Co. Kansas as the Home Extension Agent. On August 11, 1963 my college sweetheart, Alvin Johnson, and I were married. We spent most of our married life in Marysville, Kansas where we owned a Western Auto hardware and appliance store. Al managed the store and I taught gifted students in the Marysville school district for seventeen years.

Before I went back to teaching full time in 1983, I was busy staying at home with our five children. We were blessed with two biological and three adopted children. During the time prior to teaching full time, I did substitute teaching and went back the Kansas State University to earn my MS in Gifted Education. I retired from teaching in 1998.

After Al and I retired, we relocated to Burlington, Kansas where one daughter, son-in-law, and grandchildren lived. My daughter, Sara, and I owned and operated a custom embroidery business there for ten years. In 2008 that young family moved to Abilene, Kansas. Al and I weren't going to be left behind with no family in Burlington, so we moved to Abilene, too.

Alvin, my husband of forty-six years passed away October 15, 2009 after a lengthy struggle with multiple myeloma, bone marrow cancer.

I keep busy spending time with my children and grandchildren, as well as; volunteering, gardening, quilting, reading, traveling, and writing books

Frank Fender
IFYE to Taiwan
From Goshen, Ohio

IFYE Led to a Great Career

Without any doubt whatsoever, growing up on a farm, 4-H and, most especially being an IFYE were the key determinants of both my personal life and professional career. Life on the farm led to 4–H and 4-H led to an amazing IFYE assignment to Taiwan in 1962. To make a long story shorter, I'll focus on IFYE and the career that followed. The IFYE experience taught me that (1) I liked to travel (almost anywhere) (2) I enjoyed meeting and interacting with people of different cultures (and was pretty good at it.) (3) I could eat and drink almost anything (and did and still do) and (4) Being professionally involved in international economic and social development would be an interesting and exciting career (it was).

Immediately after returning from Taiwan I began my MS program in agricultural economics at Purdue University. My graduate assistantship employed me with the nascent Office of International Programs in Agricultural with responsibilities to assist in developing, implementing and administering various international education, technical assistance and research programs.

Following completion of my MS degree I was selected to participate in the Ford Foundation funded Purdue Fellows in Latin America Program. My wife Judy and I spent approximately 2 years in Argentina where I worked as a staff economist for the Argentine Ministry of Agriculture and Livestock, and consultant with the Ford Foundation.

Coming back to Purdue to pursue my PhD degree I resumed employment as Assistant to the Director of International Programs in Agriculture. Near the completion of my degree (but not as near as I thought) I took a job with the U.S. Department of Agriculture, Office of International Training (OIT). The primary mission of OIT was to arrange, administer and monitor academic and non-academic programs in agriculture at US Land Grant Universities for foreign students primarily funded by USAID. Soon after my arrival we initiated a series of short term training programs both in the US (often in cooperation with cooperating universities) as well as overseas. Again, it was a fantastic experience to work with students from many different countries as they pursued educational objectives essential to the development of their societies and economies. During this time I also spent approximately two years on the staff of the Board for International Food and Agricultural Development (BIFAD)) working on international human resource and institutional development issues.

Like most bureaucrats, my career experienced numerous USDA reorganizations. I spent the last several years, until my retirement in 2004, in the Foreign Agricultural Service as Director of the Food Industries Division (FID). The primary role of FID was to bring together public and private sector resources and expertise for human resource development efforts focused on opening and expanding international markets for US agricultural commodities and products.

During my IFYE directed international career I had the opportunity and pleasure of working in over 40 countries. It was a great career doing what my IFYE experience convinced me of; I liked to travel, enjoyed other cultures, could eat drink almost anything and economic and social development was a great way to make a living.

On the more personal level my international career with its travel and cultural interactions with many persons in and from several countries affirmed and reaffirmed time and time again the strength and validity of the IFYE motto "Peace through Understanding".

Written by Frank Fender, who resides in Springfield, Virginia.

Sharon Ries Brungard
IFYE to Taiwan
From Tecumseh, Michigan

I can't believe this is the 50th anniversary of our IFYE trip. It doesn't seem possible that so many years have gone by! I was married in the fall of 1963 and had two daughters: one is now forty-seven and the other is forty-three. I also have one granddaughter, who will be ten April 2012. I have been single since 1985 and have lived in Wisconsin, Michigan, Ohio, and Illinois.

In 1986 my youngest daughter and I took a trip to Ireland. We were there for six days. While there, we spent six hours each day horseback riding. We rode across a lot of the country, staying each night in one of the small hotels that dotted the countryside. The last day we rode bareback into the ocean. What great fun!

In 1988 I took my oldest daughter to Cozumel for six days of fun and relaxation in the sun. This was another great time and just what we needed.

In 2006 I accompanied my oldest daughter and my granddaughter to Montreal so that I could babysit my granddaughter while my daughter took a special yoga teacher's course. My oldest daughter teaches Ashtanga yoga and Thai massage in New York City. My youngest daughter has a pet care business in the St. Charles, Illinois area.

I've had an electrolysis business in St. Charles for twenty-eight years and I still love doing it. I'm thinking of retiring in another two years— time will tell!

IFYE has been the most wonderful experience of my life! It has given me knowledge of the world that has allowed me a perspective on life that simply being a tourist could never have given me. Actually living with Taiwanese families for five months and traveling around the world by ship with my fellow IFYEs seeing Vietnam, Colombo, Ceylon (Sri Lanka now), India, the Suez Canal, France, and the Pacific and Atlantic Oceans has given me a lifetime of wonderful memories to cherish.

Written by Sharon R. Ries Brungard, who resides in St. Charles, Illinois.

Doris Imhof Johnson

Doris lives at rural Abilene, Kansas. After her retirement as a gifted education teacher, she pursued her hobbies. These include writing, cooking, traveling, gardening, reading, antique quests, and best of all spending time with her children and grandchildren. Throughout her life, she's frequently recalled the wonderful experiences she had in 1962 as an IFYE, International Farm Youth Exchange, delegate to the Philippines. The people, sights, and opportunities of this trip have had a positive and unique influence in her life, family, community and world involvement, and teaching. This book is a "must read" about the adventures of a young farm girl amidst a vastly different and exciting culture.

Doris has co-authored with her brother, Ray Imhof, two books; which are memoirs of their mother's life. These books are *As I Remember it* and *Apron Strings and Family Ties.* Another book that Doris wrote is *Gutsy Women,* which is biographical chapters about sixteen extraordinary women who are wonderful role models for any age woman. Doris has also written a children's book, *The Cookie Crumb Trail.* It's a fast paced book about a little boy and his pet duckling.

Ray Imhof

Ray resides in Colby, Kansas. His interests are many and varied. He is on the visitor services staff at Prairie Museum of Art and History and works extensively with their vast photo and documents collection. To help promote tourism, Ray is also a part-time volunteer host at the Colby Visitor Information Center. Ray is a K-State Extension Master Gardener and spends much volunteer time working with educational horticulture projects and continuing his own horticulture education

Ray occupies his spare time with travel, genealogy, gardening, photography, reading, writing, and playing the organ. He also shares his home with his tabby cat, Matt

He has co-authored *As I Remember It* and *Apron Strings and Family Ties* with his sister, Doris Johnson. He also assisted Doris with editing and formatting *Gutsy Women* and *Philippine Experiences of a Kansas Farm Girl.*